This could not be imagined. Ukraine.

Mariia Kartashova

Chernihiv, 2022

Who am I

I was born in the Soviet Union in St. Petersburg, then it was Leningrad. My parents did not work out and my mother returned to her parents with me.

After graduating from the Odessa Institute, my mother was assigned to the Donetsk region. Then it was strict with this, you had to go and work. My childhood and youth were spent in the Donbas - a working region with a lot of heavy industry and coal mines. Very little greenery, bad air, but good earnings.

During perestroika, they simply stopped paying my mother's salary, we were starving, I fainted on the way from school. Then my mother started knitting woolen socks at night and selling them at the market on weekends, so I was introduced to commerce at an early age.

I studied well, entered the institute, but dropped out in the second year. Times were tough and we had to work. And why study if you can have a normal income from commerce. So I started trading in the market.

But times have changed and fate has thrown me to Chernihiv. There I met my future husband and we had two sons. I graduated from the institute, which I once quit, but did not work at the enterprise, but started my own business.

When the war started in 2014, my mother was in the Donbas. They persuaded her to leave only when her area was bombed. So she came to us with one bag.

For several years, we bought her a small apartment next to her husband's parents and just lived. On the eve of the war, we finally got our own house with a small garden. We dreamed that when the children grow up, then grandchildren will come to us there ...

1. The day before (On the eve)

And the day before everyone was talking about war ... Only I did not believe that the war could begin. The 21st century, civilization, we are not savages of any kind and – what for? I was sure that the war would not start. Well, there may be some rattling near the border, they would sign some kind of treaty and that would be the end of it.

Chernihiv is the northernmost regional center of Ukraine. Our town is at a distance of about 100 km from the border – a couple of hours in a tank. And it stands right on the way to the capital of Ukraine – Kyiv. An ancient town with a history of over 1200 years. It is filled with history to the brim – old temples and a rampart with cannons. At the same time it is very quiet and homely, with many parks and fountains. An ideal place to raise children as I always said to visitors.

On the eve of Lent, Kostya, my husband, with our eldest son Tikhon was going to go to the monastery to pray, to be closer to God, to spend some time together. The monastery in which they were going to go is located in the Sumy region – Glinskaya hermitage, in the forest 5 km from the border with Russia. Once we went there to live with my husband when we asked God for children. When Kostya asked if he should go or not, I answered with a little irritation: "Oh, come on, at least you don't escalate, go for God's sake, there will be no war". And they went early in the morning taking only a pair of spare pants as a three-day trip was planned.

New sneakers for spring had already arrived in my store as it began to get warmer early and people began to change their shoes. "Wonderful! – I thought. – It will be a good season; I will be able to earn money and repair the bathroom and install the city sewer". Just this year the city implemented a project in our district. The shop was small and divided for two owners. There was a central entrance, which was opened by the neighbors, and we had a door to the courtyard for all sorts of personal needs. The key to the back door was usually either with me or with the second seller. The following day was not my shift and I decided to leave this key just in the locker for the other guy to pick it up in the morning. If the delivery of goods or urgent shipments were supposed to be in the morning or evening, then we took the key and brought it home. But there were no urgent matters or deliveries for the morning...

 In the evening Nikon and I went to our friend's birthday party, had fun, drank tea, ate a cake, everything was the same – as always. One of our friends who fought in the east back in 2014 received a phone call and when he hung up he said: "This is it, guys, within 48 hours there would be an open attack by Russia". Anna and I looked at each other and smiled. He talked a lot about war since his return, and we thought that this was some of his chatter again which, frankly, bored us. Anna was with me, she was married to Kostya's younger brother, but they divorced. Kostya's brother Yura had been working in Odessa, on the Black Sea coast, for almost a year. Anna had to go to Kyiv in the morning for a shift at work, and she was also not going to change her plans. Her son Mikhail was already 12 years old, and he was a completely independent boy. But when his mother left for a shift, he often came to his grandmother Galya (Kostya's mother) – all the same, it's calmer when there is an adult nearby.

 We also walked a little with our friends and went home with Nikon. My younger son Nikon is a very active boy with an attention deficit. And doing lessons with him is some kind of torture. While he writes one line in a notebook, I will find out how the boy Kolya joked, what kind of beetle was outside the window and whether there are spots in the sun. And of course I get annoyed, it seems to me that being able to write is more important than beetles, and you need to write beautifully, regardless of what the boy Kolya said. Very soon I will find out that it is much more important that your child is alive even without knowing mathematics and in general it doesn't matter how he wrote if he is gone ...

Coming out of the shower and standing on the cool floor, I was annoyed again – Soviet paranoids! The fact is that our house was built after the Second World War during the Cold War with America. And the first owner who built this house was afraid of a nuclear strike and decided to make himself a shelter. As a result, over our kitchen and bathroom there is a layer of reinforced concrete of some crazy brand that no grinder would operate, rail ceilings, very thick concrete walls. There was even an emergency exit manhole, in our time it was closed with a wooden board, and a bunker for food storage. When we moved in, I wanted to make a heated floor in the bathroom, but the specialist said that he could not cut grooves there for laying the floor heating cable, I was very annoyed. Who needs a bunker in a modern house? A modern house needs underfloor heating! But, the repair had to be postponed, as there was not enough money for a more serious repair.

We used to live in an apartment in another area of the town, closer to the rampart, a 30-minute walk distance. But a year ago my husband and I made the final decision that we want to live and grow old in this town. And we bought a house. For the first time in 40 years of my life, I had my own house. I planted a garden for the first time and planned to repair the path on the street. Mentally repainted the fence and decorated the flower bed. I planned that when the children grow up and move away, their children, my grandchildren, will come to their rooms. It was all real, it was my life, which I liked and which I planned to live happily ever after. When we moved to a private house, I began to sleep very well, not like in an apartment. A quiet area near the small river Strizhen, where there are a lot of ducks in winter, because the river does not freeze. Unlike in an apartment, here everyone has their own room, and I can just rest with a book. Near the house there is a small garden, now covered with light snow in February, and still a large barn for bicycles, scooters, roller skates and other necessary things that boys value so much. My cat did not reconcile with the move and regularly ran away to the old area for a walk. I turned off the heating and lay down under the covers – the house remained warm all night through.

2. The Beginning

That morning began, as always, with my annoying alarm clock. How I hate getting up at 7 am – it's not my time at all! I turned it off and stretched out from under the blanket – it's cool, I need to turn on the heating. Sipping a cup of coffee, I checked my Facebook feed, there were several messages about war and about explosions. I snorted again and even wrote a comment under one post that everything was quiet in Chernihiv. I tried to call my mother, but for some reason she didn't pick up the phone, but I didn't attach any importance to this, maybe she's in the bathroom, maybe in the kitchen and didn't hear my call. It was later that I realized that we simply did not have a connection in the lowland, because a lot of people called their relatives that morning.

 I woke up Nykon, we had breakfast and got ready to go to flute and guitar lessons at the local School of the Arts. Jackets, hats, boots, scarf and guitar were in the case. All these things had to be put on and tied up – wintertime! Tom, the dog, sat and looked at me with devoted eyes, waiting for the command "Home" or "With me." I thought it over. Realizing that the dog would have to wait for us somewhere, I said "Home". Tom immediately drooped and even lowered his ears, but continued to sit and watch us packing.

When we crossed the river my phone picked up a signal, my mother got through to me and said that the war had begun. But even at that moment I didn't believe in a full-scale invasion, I reassured her that most likely these were pinpoint strikes on military targets, now they would achieve their goal, they would sign an agreement and that's it. Well, why in fact Russia needs Ukraine for? What do they lack on the sixth part of the land? Logically, this is a completely pointless exercise. I'm still looking for logic…

 I called the flute teacher and he said that there would be no class that day, he told us to rest and then he would call us. I shrugged my shoulders looking at Nykon in a hat jacket and with a guitar and a flute in the case. O! Our guitar lesson! When I called the guitar teacher, he was hurrying to school and said that knew nothing. Then he called back and said that the school was closed that day, "we'll call you later".

"Well, Nykon, it looks like you are having a day off today, - I told him. – Let's go walk our dog Tom and visit grandma Olya". Tom was delighted that we returned for him. While we were walking to my mother, anxiety began to cover me. There was something in the air, in the glances of hurrying people. The same yards and houses, I walked here a thousand times, but for some reason the atmosphere was different. When I was crossing the street there were people queuing to get to ATMs and to buy cigarettes. Something stirred in my soul, something bad, something disturbing. But I reassured myself that they are alarmists, they do not live like a normal human being – and went on.

A salesperson from my store phoned.

– What will we do, Mariia Mikhailovna?

– And what can you do, Dmitry Valerievich? Stay at home, get orders but warn our customers that delivery may be delayed. That's all we can do so far. If nothing changes, go to work in the afternoon and send the goods.

– Where is the key to the warehouse?

 – ***, the key to the warehouse is in the warehouse. Okay, wait, I'll think of something. I called the owner of the second department. Of course, they were not going to open the store that day. If you need the key, you need to go to another area of the town, but so far it doesn't seem necessary. It's not urgent, that's for sure.

My best friend Lena, godmother of my youngest child, lived next to my mother's block of flats. Her apartment was on the way to my mom so I decided to go to Lena first, because I couldn't get through in the morning. We went upstairs and called.

 When Lena opened the door, I was very surprised: her children were dressed, their shoes were on and there were bags with things on the doorstep. "Where are you going?!" – I exclaimed. "What do mean – where? To you! You have a shelter!"

For several seconds we stood opposite each other in absolute silence, comprehending the situation. "Well, okay", – I thought. – "Lena used to come to visit me with her children, nothing unusual". Except for a bunch of stuff and Archie, the dog, which they took with them.

– Pack up. I'll go to my mother's and off we go.

Going out into the street, I noticed a family who were loading things into the car – they were in a hurry. And two women and a small boy walked past me. The kid was almost running not being able to keep up with the hurrying adults. Then the thought flashed through my mind for the first time: "Maybe I need to leave too?" But, I shook my head, it will end soon, why running back and forth?

Mom, as always, met us with a laid table. It was before having children that I was picky about food, and after their birth the absence of the necessity to cook food is already a holiday. "Of course, we will eat!" – I said to Nikon, and told my mother that she was going to go to us, our place was much quieter and there was a shelter.

"I won't go anywhere," my mother answered, "here is my house and I see no reason to run away. We lived near Donetsk for months under the howl of sirens and nothing happened". "I have deja vu!" – I exclaimed chewing buckwheat. In 2014, when the conflict in eastern Ukraine was just beginning, my mother lived in the Donetsk region. I immediately told her to come to us to Chernihiv, but she tried to excuse herself saying that everything would be fine, that there was no need to be afraid. When the war reached her city near Donetsk, she left under fire, their train was fired upon and all the passengers were transferred to the front four cars, they went jammed all the way to Kyiv.

– Will you then run under the shots?

– It's not far to run from here ... Okay, Masha, don't push me, everything will be fine. Go with Lena, if they shoot, which I doubt, I will come.

We also went to the apartment next to where Kostya's parents lived. They also shrugged their shoulders and said that there was no need to panic, thanked for the invitation and said that they would stay at home so far. They could not believe that the Russians, whom we considered to be brothers, would bomb our cities.

We returned to Lena. By this time, they had already prepared their trunks, things, and we set off on our way home. It was not far to go, but given that we had four children, two dogs and a stroller loaded with things, we walked for probably an hour. On the way, we could see a lot of people hurrying somewhere, there were queues in the shops. I told Lena almost at the house:

– Go home, Nikon will open the door, and I will run to the store.

When I entered the store, I saw such a long line (about 50 people) that I realized that I would be standing there for a long time. But I decided that I had no choice. People in panic will sort out all the products and I will not even have bread and milk for the children for dinner. I stood in that line and started to listen to the conversations. People discussed where you could buy groceries, where you could still withdraw money, where there were cigarettes sold, which road was better to take if you wanted to leave the town. But 10 minutes later the saleswoman caught our attention and said that the store was closing, sorry. People were displeased but although they grumbled, they began to go outside.

I returned home and told Lena that the stores were like this now. I assigned them a place in the hall, laid out a sofa and an armchair so that they could rest if necessary. I took out food and asked Lena to cook something for lunch because it was already about eleven. And she took money from her backpack and went in search of food. Although I still didn't believe that there would be a full-scale war and that there would be some delays with food, I decided to buy supplies at least for a couple of days just in case – we had children, after all. The two nearest stores were closed, which seemed strange to me – well, how can you deprive people of the opportunity to buy food in times like this? The third one was open. There were queues in each department; I took a queue in three departments at once – bread, fish and dairy. I also wanted to take a turn in the meat department, but it turned out that they had run out of food. I bought coffee and tea, not my favorite, but the one they had. There was no bread at all, even yesterday's bun was not there, I bought cookies – that was at least something. I bought a pack of pasta and some fish that would be more suitable for cats than for us. This is an indescribable feeling when you choose products in the store from those that are available, because those that you need are not available at all.

While I was standing in line, Anna called me and very anxiously asked what was going on. She had left for Kyiv to work as planned.

– I don't even know what's going on here. Lena came to me with her children because we have a shelter, I don't know what will happen next.

– May Misha come to you? – Anna asked.

– Of course! It's not even a question. I'm sorry that I didn't remember and didn't offer it myself. – I answered. Thank God there is enough room for everyone.

Approaching the house, I saw a neighbor from the neighboring part of the house, Yulia, she looked out of the window when she saw me.

– Hi! What are you? What's up? – I asked immediately.

– Oh I do not know! – Yulia exclaimed. – Yura called, said that I should pack my things, there would be an evacuation. Will you be leaving?

- No. This is where my home will be for now. If you go out, at least come in and tell me, maybe you can leave the keys to the house. You never know what may come.

Arriving home, we ate and went out into the yard for the children to run around. We drank coffee and chatted. Everything was as always, as if the godmother just came to visit us and we are drinking coffee, and the children are fussing around.

Suddenly we heard the growing howl of air raid alert. This howl causes goosebumps and we fell into a stupor for a few seconds, as well as the children, and then screamed: -"Quickly to the shelter!" We helped the children go down and went down ourselves. It's good that the children were outdoors and well-dressed, because it was cold in the basement. It should be cold, because it is made for storing food and vegetables. Since it was the first time, we just sat and did not move, the children also sat frozen and only looked around with frightened little eyes. Everyone was frozen in anticipation of something terrible. But minutes passed and nothing terrible happened. The children slowly began to thaw, tugging at each other and laughing. I got out of the basement and went to the courtyard to look. Everything around was as always, the wind stirred the tops of the trees, the birds flew from branch to branch, somewhere the neighbor's cat was screaming.

– Get out. It's quiet here, – I called into the basement. The children ran out into the yard in a joyful crowd. Elena came out and we began to discuss what had happened. We understood that we weren't ready.

– We need to carry a warm blanket there and something to sit on, a laptop so that the children will have something to do, maybe water and some snacks, who knows how long the air raid alarm will last next time. Neighbor Yulia appeared from behind the fence:

– How are you?

– Well, we just got into the bunker to see what it must be equipped with, – I answered a little humorously. Back then it still seemed like an adventure, like active tourism.

– Do you have a normal basement? Because we have just a cellar that is covered with boards.

– Oh! We have a real bunker! If it's scary, come to us and sit here, I'll leave the gate open, if anything happens, feel free to run here.

We took out the mattresses which were lying there in case something happened from the barn and the spare pillows were all brought as well. An extension cord and a laptop were brought too so that the children could watch cartoons. I packed my documents in my backpack and put them into the basement as well. We also brought a small heater there to warm the room a little.

When Mikhail came about an hour later, just at that moment the siren also began to howl.

– Come in quickly, don't undress, go down to the basement, – I told him.

Julia looked out:

– Well, what about us?

– Come to us, we should stay close.

A minute later Julia came running with both children and a potty for the youngest. We went down to the basement and switched cartoons for the children. Tom ran around the hatch into the basement, but did not go down. I desperately called him and tried to persuade him to go down with us, but he ran away as soon as I wanted to take him in my arms. I had to leave him outside. The basement had a large trapdoor made of thick boards and a plank grate that we put up in the summer so that the cold air from the basement would cool the kitchen. I closed the entrance only to the grate so that Tom could see us. He calmed down and lay down near the entrance.

We sat down with the girls on the mattress and started talking to get a little distraction from what was happening. When twenty minutes passed, I got out of the basement to check, went out into the yard and heard explosions somewhere in the distance. As it turned out later, our guys blew up bridges to slow down the advance of the Russians. Around the same time, planes were flying and bombing the airfield "Pevtsy" near Chernigov. This was the first time I heard explosions, at that time they were like firecrackers, I still didn't know whether it was to us or from us, whether it was a mine or a plane, just pops.

When I decided that it was safe, I told the girls and children about it. Yulia and the children went back to her room to continue getting ready and waiting for her husband. Lena and I started preparing dinner.

Kostya called and told me that on the highway not far from the monastery, where he was with Tykhon, Russian tanks passed early in the morning, and now they are behind the front lines. But everything is quiet there; the usual monastic life goes on with its service, meal, prayer, obedience. Kostya suggested returning to Chernigov. But on reflection, we decided that it was too dangerous for a man of military age to cross the front line in the most acute phase, it is not known who will shoot him: our own soldiers or the others. And if something happens to Tykhon, then my heart will stop beating in my chest.

– Stay there and pray for two, three days. We'll see what will happen, - I was sure that everything would end quickly and they would come home.

Yulia's husband, Yura, returned from work and said that there would be no evacuation as it was too late for that. The siren wailed again. I can't express what it feels like when you hear this howl, when you understand that now planes are flying here that they will shoot missiles and you don't know where they will shoot. Perhaps their target is located near your house, perhaps the pilot will miss, or perhaps they will deliberately throw a bomb in your direction. Along with the beginning of the siren, a chill comes down your back, but at the same time, confusion goes away and some kind of composure and knowledge of what must be done comes.

After Yura sat with us and his family in our shelter, he said:

– It won't do!

He stuffed all the holes with rags, even the emergency exit hole, so that he could get it out but so that the air would not pass now.

– Do you have a big heater? - He asked.

– It's in the warehouse somewhere. Let's go and search.

We went and got a bigger heater, brought another tee, brought it all into the basement. Julia brought more blankets and rugs from her house and we began to equip our shelter. When we turned on the big heater, the lights went out. At first, everyone was afraid that the power lines had been damaged from the explosions and the light had completely disappeared. But then it turned out that the plugs could not withstand the stress. Strongly powerful oil accumulator and old wiring are not compatible.

Yura installed two ladders on both sides of the fence so that he could quickly climb from their yard to ours. But when they got over the fence with the children, they decided to stay overnight in our house. Because climbing over the fence under the howl of a siren with sleeping children is another quest. I put them in Nykon's room when they brought another mattress. And so they got two beds for four people (two adults and two children). Nykon decided to sleep with me on the bed, and Misha was given Tykhon's room. Sleep came quickly caused by the tiredness after the day. But not for long, they really started bombing us....

3. Day Two

We were woken up at about one in the morning by the sound of sirens and explosions. At night, when the whole city was asleep, the explosions were heard very strongly. It felt like bombs were falling in a neighboring yard. Although in reality it was the outskirts of Chernigov that were bombed. We jumped out of bed, picked up the children and carried them to the shelter. Nykon was capricious:

– Mom, I want to sleep.

I got mad at him, I even said something rude. When I thought that I could lose my own child, for some reason I felt not tenderness, but anger. Helped Lena bring her three children down. It's good that Rada, the eldest, woke up almost immediately and helped

Katya and me. At the age of 9, Rada generally behaved like an adult. She helped her mother with her youngest daughter in everything, it was so unexpected. We lowered the children into the sleepy basement, and it was very cold there. I woke up Misha, in my opinion, he didn't understand at all what was happening, just sleepy, he went where they led him, while he was going down to the basement, he almost fell, it's good that Yura was below and picked him up. Yulia and I rushed upstairs, grabbed our jackets and a few blankets, quickly, without further ado, threw them down, went down ourselves and closed the hatch. The children grumbled, cried and acted up, and we began to dress them in clothes and wrap them in a blanket. I couldn't stop thinking: "Have I forgotten anything?"

The shelter was quiet, the sounds of distant explosions did not reach here. The children began to go to bed right as they were on top of each other, and after 15 minutes there was silence and a sleepy kingdom.

– Well what are we going to do? – I asked the adults.

– We will sleep here with the children, – Yura said.

– I'll sleep here too, who knows how many more times I'll have to run at night… – Lena decided.

I sat with them for another 20 minutes and went upstairs. She left only Nykon and Mikhail downstairs, why drag the child back and forth? I sleep very badly in unfamiliar surroundings, and I need strength. There were no more explosions outside, I climbed into bed and instantly fell asleep...

– Maria, get up! Air Alert! I decided to wake you up, - Yura bothered me.

– Yes, yes. I'm coming.

I got off the bed and followed him. I slept in my clothes, so I didn't have to pack. A siren wailed through the town, but no explosions were heard. It was later that we learned that the siren is turned on when the radars spotted enemy aircraft, but if the air defense works well, then the plane is shot down before approaching the town. We went down to the basement, the children slept peacefully, Lena too. It was about 5 o'clock in the morning. So, I didn't want to get up at 7 by the alarm clock, now I get up by the siren at 5!

– Did you sleep? – I asked Yura and Yulia.

– I dozed a little... – he pointed to the corner in which they were sitting, all wrapped in winter clothes and blankets and with children in their arms. – Its hard to fall asleep here...

– Yeah...We need to prepare another room in the shelter. Clean up the mess and bring in another mattress to the second room of the shelter. They are bombing the outskirts. It's only a matter of time before they reach the center of town.

I climbed outside, and Yura and Yulia decided to try to take a nap. I turned on the heating, because the house began to cool down in the morning and brewed some coffee.

It started to get light. I went outside with a cup of coffee and listened. In the far north, I heard some clapping, which we couldn't identify. Maybe our artillery was advancing on Russian positions?They could not approach the town because of the blown up bridges.

I decided to bake pancakes for everyone, since I woke up anyway. Taking out flour and sugar, I realized that these would be the last pancakes if I did not find a working store. There are a lot of us now, what I bought yesterday ended yesterday, I didn't have large stocks of food. What I had was for about 3-5 days for 4 people, but there were already 11 of us (4 adults and 7 children).

And let's not forget about two dogs, two cats and a hamster! Feeding them all would be a miracle. For the animals, I had food for a week.

At that moment mum phoned me. My early bird!

– How are you?

– Fine. Just making pancakes. Having trouble finding supplies.

– I can bring you some potatoes. You just brought me two bags, remember?

– That would be great! How will you get here? Can you walk?

– Yes, I'll try to go to the store on the way to you.

– Ok. Please be careful.

I was planning to lure my mother here under the pretext of potatoes. When she arrived I would insist she stayed with me where it was safer.

Even with bombs dropping it was still safer to be away from high-rise buildings.

My attention turned to Lena who had spent most of the day engrossed in her phone .

– Get off the phone and sit with me. I need attention too.

– I need to know what's going on, it's important. They say they took Gorodnya (a city north of Chernihiv), people post videos of tanks driving through the streets! They are going to Chernihiv!

– Put down the phone, – I said gently, – You will have a nervous breakdown if you keep reading the news. What then will I do with you?

– Vitya phoned (Lena's husband). He says his workshop in the basement was full of people, and they spent the night. He is in a panic, he has musical instruments there and tools to repair them. He asks if he can come to you, and he will leave Gosha in the workshop.

– Yes, he certainly may! – I replied. "Did they even need to ask?"

Vitya arrived on a bicycle, the children had already woken up and joyfully rushed to him crying:

– Daddy, Daddy!

Yura immediately put him to work. They pulled an extension cord from Yura's house and plugged in a large heater in the hideout. But it was still cold and damp there, the basement eventually warmed up somewhere on the fourth day with the condition of constant operation of two heaters.

We had breakfast and drank tea as we woke up.

Sister called from Russia:

– Maria, I'm sorry! We didn't know it would go this far! What a nightmare! People come out to protest, but they are dispersed. How are you?

– Everybody is alive so far. They're bombing. We are in the basement.

– Can I help you?

– No... But it would be nice if you could call sometimes so I know you're ok. Right now we need the support of our families. Don't get sucked into hatred, alright?

– Yes, I don't support it. All my friends are against the war, but they can't do anything about it.

So...They can't do anything and we can't do anything. Why are our cities being bombed if neither side wants war?

– Dad is coming now, can he? – Julia came up.

– Yes. Everything is fine?

– I went to the draft board in the morning, I wanted to sign up as a volunteer. They said – disperse, there are no weapons for you.

The siren sounded. Everyone ran downstairs. Since the children were in the house and undressed, they quickly left their jackets there. Yulya's dad came, there was something to listen to. He is an officer, in the past a military man, now he is over 60 years old, but with current circumstances he decided to take up arms and defend his homeland. Almost two hundred people came to the military enlistment office, but all the weapons were handed out yesterday. It turns out that on the first day of the war, many men have already come ready to defend their city and ready to die for their country. One guy walked 20 km from a neighboring village, walked all night, and was told to go back. Dad left the remote area of Chernihiv at 6 in the morning to be at the military registration and enlistment office at 8, now he had the same two hours to go back.

– Can you stay?

– No, I need to meet my wife, my soul mate, she's in another shelter, I need to go sit with her.You have no room here anyway, – and went to his house as soon as the air raid ended.

The buyer called, claiming that his order had not been shipped since yesterday. They were simply not bombed yet and everything worked for them, and it was not clear to him why people did not take his order to the post office. I promised to find out if the Post Office was working. But I have another problem, I can not get into the store to pick up the sold goods. How to get to another area to take the key to the store in the absence of public transport? It so happened that our car was just in the workshop. And I also told Kostya to take it. But he said he would come and take it as I didn't need it. It turned out I needed it!

Mom Olya came with potatoes:

– I didn't get into the store – everything is closed. What do you need to cook for dinner? – she was ready to act for the benefit of the family.

– Oh, I have a pot of borshch in the fridge, – Julia said and brought a large pot of national Ukrainian dish. So we had a large pot to cook for a large number of people. Because all of mine were 3 liters only designed for our family.

After lunch, since it was quiet, I decided to go to the post office and find out if it was working because I could not get through to them in the morning. I got on my bike and drove to the central avenue. I haven't pedaled like that for a long time, the bike stood as a last resort, and now this extreme case has come. I was driving very fast, as an air raid alert could start at any moment. There was practically no one on the streets. There were checkpoints at the crossroads in the center. Several concrete slabs (where did they get them from?) and two soldiers from the Territorial Defense with machine guns. They stopped every car and checked the documents. I was haunted by a feeling of unreality, as if I was watching a simple action movie. There was a fear that they would stop me too, but I did not take any documents, but they did not stop me, I drove past, trying not to look in their direction. I saw people leaving the grocery store.

– Is the shop open? – I asked the guard.

– We're closing.

– Can you let me in? Should I at least get some milk for the kids?

– No milk. There is almost nothing. Come tomorrow at 8 am, we will open.

– Excellent! Thank you! – I happily replied and drove on. Cool, I'll buy more food tomorrow.

I drove up to my store.Above the entrance hung a new blue SPORTOBUV sign, made only two months ago according to the new city standards. These were free-standing luminous raised letters - very beautiful and very expensive. To write the name of the store in English letters, it was necessary to apply for trademark registration, and I did it. It's high time, the store is already 11 years old. Yes, yes, next year I will become the owner of the sportobuv trademark, and what should I do with it now...

The shutter on the window and on the door was intact, the alarm peephole blinked cheerfully. I wonder if security will come if the alarm goes off? Can you ship items home? After all, so much effort and energy has been invested, but you don't know where the projectile will hit, in a store or in a house? Maybe if the house is destroyed, then I can live in the store?

I looked around the corner at the post office. It turned out that the post office was closed, there were no announcements on the doors either, I only had to wait. I turned my bike around and rode home at full speed. A little out of shape, my legs ached and refused to pedal at high speed. But I still pressed through, because I really wanted to go home.

Driving up to the house, I met neighbors at the corner, everyone left the houses as if to attend a rally. We moved not so long ago and I still didn't know who lived nearby.

I saw Yura and he came up to tell me what was happening. We are trying to help the defenders of the town, he explained.

They needed old tires from cars to block the intersections in case tanks drove into the town. They also needed glass bottles and fabric to make "Molotov cocktails..." or petrol bombs as they are also called. It helped people feel useful and empowered, to take action and not just sit in the basement.

If now they were told to dig trenches, they would run to take shovels and run to dig - there were no indifferent people. There was already a pile of building materials and a couple of crates of glass bottles on the corner.

– And where do you leave supplies? – I asked Yura.

– The guys from the Territorial Defense will come and take them away. I already called them.

When I entered the yard, I saw that my yard was a mess.

The children who were let out for a walk in the yard and were bored decided to dig up my yard for fun. But since they are children, they dug in pieces in different places. As a result, everything was in the pits and all the children were in the mud. Jackets, hats, shoes, everything was one solid lump of mud.

My thinking about all that mess was interrupted by shots. The children ran to the house, but I stood on the threshold with open arms.

– No entrance in muddy clothes! Take them off!

If they smeared everything in the shelter, then it would be difficult to clean it. Yura came running and helped to take off the children's clothes. Everyone quickly undressed and went down to the shelter, and before that I threw everything into the bathroom – I'll figure it out later. The children turned on the cartoon and began to listen. Shots were heard, but there was no air raid warning, and this confused us.

When the sounds of gunshots stopped, we began to share the news. I told about the things I saw in the city, and Yura told what he heard from his neighbors: they created a group in Viber where they were going to share the news and if someone needs help, you can immediately write there. From the defense of the town they asked for a blackout. That is, when it gets dark, the lights must be turned off everywhere, so that it would be harder for the enemy to direct artillery and aircraft. And the town has a curfew from 8 pm to 6 am, during which it is forbidden to move around the town without special permission. We talked a little longer and then climbed outside.

Somehow everyone found something to do, everyone understood what needed to be done. Olya's mother started to cook dinner, for such a large number of people took time and effort, but she enthusiastically set to work. I helped her a little and went to wash the children's shoes and outerwear. It was necessary to do this carefully, since Lena's children did not have spare shoes, and, besides, I could not afford to spend a lot of water.

Lena and Yulia were setting up the shelter in preparation for the night, they were going to spend it downstairs with the children again. It was still cold and damp there despite the two heaters, because it was winter and although the sun was already peeking out during the day, it was cold. We lowered almost all the blankets that I had in the house there to lay them on the floor. The floor was very cold. And the walls near the children's bed were lined with pillows so that the cold would come less from the wall. They vacated the second room and laid the mattress there as well.

Finally got through to Kostya.

– Well, how are you?

– Somewhere in the distance explosions are heard, but they are not loud. I approached the rector, he allowed us to stay with Tykhon for as long as needed. He prayed for us that we would be safe and read Psalm 90 and Psalm 26. How are you?

– Fine. Setting up a cellar, – I told the news and again complained that I did not pick up the car - I need to go for the key to the store in another area. How?

– I'll ask a friend, he will take you, just call in the morning. What else can you say? Tykhon here made friends with dogs and a donkey in the barnyard. Feels good, only eats poorly. Well, take care of yourself.

It got dark. We put out the lights everywhere, left only in the hallway so that it would be a little brighter in the kitchen. The siren howled again, and again everyone descended into the shelter as quickly as possible. Dinner was ready and we lowered our plates of food into the hideout. It was very strange and not convenient to eat squatting and grinding to each other. The children had something falling off their plates, but we just silently picked it up. They ate in silence, everyone was hungry, and even Nykon, for whom food was always difficult to eat without prompting.

 Plates were collected in a pile and simply put at their feet. They began to put the children to bed, Lena read them a book, and they lay in bed with each other almost without moving. We had two mattresses one for each room in the shelter. The double bed was shared by the children. All 7 were bundled into it with two adults either side to stop them rolling onto the floor. The other room had a single mattress which was shared by two adults.

Mom and I went upstairs. Lena persuaded us that they would make room, but I decided that in case of danger I would go down, and now I need to get a good sleep. Mom didn't want to trade comfortable sleep for safety either. We also washed the dishes with her, fed the animals and went to bed. I took off only the top jacket and socks, so that in case of anything I could immediately run. Tom, as always, settled down at my feet, and I shoved Tenya under the covers, he was a living heating pad for me. I set my alarm for 6 in the morning so that I could go to the grocery store at 7. Of course, I didn't need it...

4. Trip around the city.

Of course, I didn't need an alarm clock. At 5 o'clock I woke up from the sound of gunshots. I was beginning to slowly get used to them and understand the idea that they weren't shooting at us, they were shooting at our soldiers. But since I was awake anyway, I got up and went to the kitchen. My mother was already awake and busy, cleaning and washing the worktops.

 – Good morning. Can't sleep?

 – Well, of course I can't sleep, it's a new place and the sound of gunshots is indescribable. Would you like some coffee? I've already boiled the kettle.

 – Yes, please, – I said, scratching behind the ear of Tom the cat, who followed me.

We drank coffee, discussed what supplies we needed from the store and at 06:30 I got ready to go to the queue at the store. But the air raid broke my plans. It was clear that in response to the work of our artillery, an answer from the enemy would now arrive and the answer would just be in Chernihiv, so we went to sit underground. Everyone was sleeping peacefully there, only Yulia opened her eyes and nodded her head to ask what was happening out there.

I waved my hand back gently telling her to go back to sleep. We didn't have to say anything out loud, everything was clear anyway. We just sat in the basement of the house, and somewhere on the outskirts a village was being bombed... A lot of houses were damaged, people died, many people sitting in the basement, like us, were littered, many lost their homes. Among the victims were our friends.

Half an hour later, when the shelling of Chernihiv ended, I got ready and went to the store. When I approached, there was already a line of 50 people near the store.

 Well, I had no choice except to stand, I needed food for the kids and I didn't know any other shops that were open. After about half an hour of standing in line, an air siren howled. And it was really scary there. When you are at home, even on the street in the courtyard of the house, you feel at least somehow protected, but here, at the intersection of large streets in the city center, it felt like you were standing in the middle of the city completely naked.

I think everyone felt the same because people began to look around and shift from foot to foot, but no one left. Most likely everyone else was running low on supplies and had little choice but to stay. And we all stood shifting and looking around in anticipation that something terrible might happen.

In the following days, the worst did happen in Chernihiv when a shell fell next to the queue to the store, many people died. But this day, God had mercy, after 10 minutes the air raid alarm stopped and we calmly stood until the store opened.

About 20 people were let into the store at once, and then they let them take turns, one goes out, one comes in, so that there is no crush inside the store. When I entered and walked through the store, I felt confused.

Most of what we needed was taken, there was no flour, sugar, milk again. But there was bread, only it didn't look like normal baked goods. I supposed it was probably baked from a mixture of different flours, both white and black, and they were just shapeless loaves.

The store refused to give out more than three so I took them, and some cookies I found, some sour cream (instead of milk), some canned goods, sunflower oil and butter.

When I got to the checkout it turned out they only accepted cash and didn't have card readers! It was a huge disappointment for people who had waited for hours as they had to leave the store empty handed.

When I got home everyone was already awake. Mom cooked what she could with our meager supplies and the girls minded and washed the children. Nykon ran up to me:

– Mum, where have you been? There was a siren, I was afraid that they would kill you there! He pressed his whole body against me.

–Well, that wont happen, – I reassured him. – Let them just try to throw a bomb at me! I'll take a big bat and whack it back to them! – I joked with him.

I phoned one of my friends who had a car. I needed a favor. I needed to go into the city for a key! He told me he would be there within the hour, but within the hour the city began to be very heavily bombed, shells fell within the city centre.

They blew up the building of the SBU. Explosions were heard even in the shelter, and then, probably for the first time, I took the prayer of words and gathered everyone for prayer. I read the 90th psalm and everyone around repeated, here is its text:

1 He who dwells under the roof of the Most High rests under the shadow of the Almighty,

2 says to the Lord, "My refuge and my protection, my God, in whom I trust!"

3 He will deliver you from the snare of the hunter, from the deadly sore,

4 He will hide you behind His shoulders, and under His wings you will hope; His truth will surround you as a weapon.

5 Thou shalt not be afraid of terrors in the night, of an arrow flying by day,

6 A pestilence that walks in darkness, a plague that devastates at noon.

7 A thousand will fall at your side, and ten thousand at your right hand; but it won't come close to you,

8 You will only look with your eyes and see the retribution of the wicked.

9 For you said, "The Lord is my hope"; You have chosen the Most High as your refuge;

10 Evil will not happen to you, and the plague will not come near your dwelling.

11 for he will command his angels concerning you to guard you in all your ways:

12 They will carry you in their hands, lest you strike your foot against a stone.

13 you will step on the asp and the basilisk; you will trample on the lion and the dragon.

14 "Because he loved me, I will deliver him; I will protect him, because he knows my name.

15 He will call to me, and I will hear him; I am with him in sorrow; I will deliver him and glorify him,

16 with length of days I will satisfy him, and I will show him my salvation."

Many of us considered ourselves believers, but it was then that we learned what it meant to sincerely turn to God.

My friend phoned and said:

– Sorry, my relatives won't let me come to drive you.

– Yes, I understand, – I answered. It's far to dangerous to go in.

Customers called again asking about the delivery of shoes. I told them to be patient and added that on Monday everything would work out, because I believed so. I still believed that on Monday everything would be fine.

When this nightmare ended, mother Galya called and asked if she could come to us with her friend Aunt Tanya. Aunt Tanya lived alone, the area in which she lived was in the north of the city and she was very scared.

– Sure, come, there's enough room for everyone, – I replied. They came about half an hour after the end of the air raid alert. Aunt Tanya brought her cat Milka with her. I gave them Tykhon's room, laid out a bed there and told them where they could get something if needed.

It was evident that Aunt Tanya was very shy, she did not feel confident. I tried my best to show and tell her where everything was in the house, how to use water, where to get cups and spoons, gave them pillows and blankets so that she could feel as comfortable as possible.

In the hall we had a large TV, but it was not connected to the antenna. This was done intentionally so as not to waste free time on TV programs. We used it just as an output device, I downloaded movies to the SD card, inserted it into the TV and we watched if there was something interesting.

Now I downloaded good old movies that our grandmothers loved so much to the SD card. She suggested that they turn it on and watch when they were bored.

I gave the cat Milka a bowl and a box of toilet roll and placed them in the room. We decided to keep Milka in the room for now, because I have a dog and a cat in my house and it is not known how she will react to them and how they will react to her.

We did not let Lena's dog Archik into the house, because the cat Shadow attacked him. Once Rada felt sorry for Archik during the shelling and let him into the house. Tom reacted calmly, and the Shadow rushed to his face and scratched his nose. After that, we equipped him with a booth near the front door and he lived there, they let him into the house only for the night in the kitchen when I took Shadow to my room.

While I was instructing grandmother Galya and grandmother Tanya, I reminded once again the girls with children that I do not have a city sewer, only a cesspool. And you need to be very careful with water, because if the pit overflows, finding someone to empty it would be challenging…

We made a joint decision to wash the dishes in a basin, so less water should be consumed. We also started to use the outdoor toilet, no one had used it for a long time, but we cleaned it and asked the adults during the day to try to use it to save water.

Lena and I were drinking coffee on the street, we had an interesting conversation about the whole scenario.

– … imagine you went to the outside toilet and a rocket hit the toilet and our limbs got blasted off and we got covered in waste.

– What a horrible thought! – Lena exclaimed.

– Horrible, yes ... But anything can happen. Please, promise me that if this happens to me, you will wash me before burial.

– Why are you saying all this crap?

– You know... I'm not sure myself anymore. So many crazy things are happening right now. Things I thought to be impossible. I know it's crazy but just promise me.

And we promised each other that if such an unlikely situation did happen, then we would wash each other's remains and bury them as expected, and not in shit.

To anyone reading this: this probably sounds like such a stupid and terrible thing to consider but at the time it seemed to us completely plausible and I needed reassurance if I died I would be washed before the burial.

Now in the house we had three grandmothers, and from that day an unspoken tradition began that they cook dinner in turn, one decides what to cook and the other two assist with preparations.

After dinner, Sasha, the friend with the car, phoned me and said that we could go into town now as things had quietened if I still needed a lift .

I replied that of course I was ready, it should have been done a long time ago. I went out to him on the road, got into the car and we drove off. He said that all of them, as a family, also moved to his brother's private house: his brother's family, his family and parents, everyone was now in a private house.

While we were driving around the city, we ran into dead ends several times: the roads were blocked with tires and concrete slabs, so that if tanks entered the city, they could not pass anywhere.

Two or three times we were stopped at a checkpoint: they asked who you were, where you were going, asked to show your Ukrainian passport. Of course, we had all necessary documents with us, it was already clear that without them going out into the street was impossible.

There were people with machine guns at the checkpoints, and a ready machine gunner was always sitting in the distance behind the bags in case the driver of the car turned out to be an enemy.

When we arrived in another district and drove into the quarter, it was a quarter of five-story houses, all the people from the houses were mostly standing at the entrances. As I understand it, they were afraid to go up to the apartments, they stood talking in the open, and when there was an alarm, they went down into the bomb shelter under the house.

I called the seller of another store, she had to go down and take out the key, she was just in the apartment. Sasha stayed in the car at the corner of a five-story building, and I went to the entrance. People who were standing near the entrance began to ask me: who I am, what I am doing here – everyone was afraid of impostors.

I tried to explain to them that I had lost my key and the seller from the other store would bring me the key but they got suspicious. I couldn't prove my story. In truth if the seller had been absent much longer it could have ended in trouble.

You can probably understand them, they were scared. There were rumors about turncoats who put marks on houses that glow in the dark and then rockets hit these targets at night.

Finally, the seller came out, I asked if it was necessary for her to return the keys today, when I pick up mine from the store, but she replied that she still doesn't need the keys now and let me keep them.

– Take care of yourself, – I replied.

She nodded in response and went to the entrance.

When I returned to the car, it turned out that Sasha's car was surrounded by men with the same questions as women asked me: who he was, what he was doing there, why he had come. Sasha was clearly frightened. But I arrived on time to help him out, I showed the key and explained to the crowd what we were doing, got into the car and we drove faster.

On the way back we were stopped several times at checkpoints. We went the other way and saw the exploded SBU building, it was on fire from the inside, I took a few photos.

On some streets there were anti-tank hedgehogs, for the first time in my life I saw such a picture with my own eyes. I was tempted to take a picture, but I didn't do it because there were checkpoints nearby and the guys might think that we were spies.

After a meeting near that five-story building, I realized that it's better not to joke with such things now, you may not have time to explain that you are just filming for history, and not for Russian intelligence. There were explosion holes on some roads, but some small ones, I don't know why, I don't understand this. There was also an interesting moment when we drove out from behind one turn, and an infantry fighting vehicle with a red cross was driving towards us at speed.

I was frightened for a moment. – Does he see us?

– He must see, – Sasha answered, – you see the head is sticking out of the hatch. Sasha pressed the car to the right and the BMP turned left and drove around us. In general, few people followed the rules of the road, and there were few cars.

I returned home safely, and there were new things in the garden again. Since I forbade digging up the garden, the children decided to build there. They took out the slats and stuck them into the ground, they made a palisade, they took out an old box from under the TV and it was their house. As they explained, they are building a defensive post. Well, thank God! Children at work, carried away means less sad thoughts.

Somehow quickly it got dark and we did not have time to cook dinner. It was somehow inconvenient to cook it under the lanterns, and I said:

– Well, let's turn on the light for half an hour.

Yura went out into the yard to see how it looked from the outside and said doomedly:

– No, it won't work like that. You need to close the windows. Do you have cardboard?

– Should be downstairs, – I answered, – go look with a flashlight.

While we were preparing dinner, the men found cardboard and barricaded both windows in the kitchen so that no light came out through them. But from that day on, we never removed the cardboard from the windows.

When it was time to go to bed, grandmothers also refused to go down to the shelter for the night. So we spent the night upstairs. The night was very restless, at about 2 o'clock in the morning very strong explosions were heard, such that the earth even shook, and in the morning we found out that the shell hit the house where dad was sleeping...

5. They bombed the city center.

Dad came at 5 am. We didn't know what happened, he just knocked on the window, went in and sat on a chair, not letting go of his dog's leash.

Dad was, of course, in shock, at the time waving his hands when he told us what happened, as if he couldn't find words for what happened. The house where he lived was hit by a rocket during the night. We assumed that they were aiming at the television tower that was next to the house.

Fortunately for us, it hit the side of the building, my parents' apartments were at the main entrance and avoided damage. Kostya's parents' apartment was just facing my mum's and avoided damage too.

The explosion happened about 2 am and dad, of course, was sleeping. "I woke up from a terrible explosion," dad explained, "the whole house was shaking, windows flew out" When he realized what had happened, he quickly put on his shoes, took the dog and went to the shelter under the house.

Almost the whole tower block had already gathered there, and dad stayed there until the morning. Under the main tower block house there was no bomb shelter, it was just a basement with rooms for each apartment, where residents kept things they did not need.

And so, in the narrow rooms of the basement, people took shelter without basics, using boxes to sit and sleep on. The building entrance was burned to the ground, only the walls remained there.

Dad continued to explain:

– I don't know if people were hurt there, but one woman from the apartment that was on fire was sitting with her dad in the basement. Where the rest of the inhabitants were, I do not know.

Dad came along with his dog named Caesar. He was a great big husky pup. He was originally a gift. Kostya brought him from the monastery to dad as a gift. The monastery used to take on strays and his previous owner didnt have time to take proper care of the dog (Huskies need walked at least 12 miles a day).

My dog Tom, of course, was in shock by the new addition. A new dog in his territory! Which... moreover, is three times larger than him. Thankfully Tom calmed down after 10 minutes and accepted the new addition.

The dogs would now need more food, especially Ceaser who ate like a horse. I decided to entrust the care of the dogs to Misha. As a teenager Misha needed to feel important and wanted to be more useful, especially when he spent much of his time feeling helpless with the other children in the basement.

We had no meat for the dogs, so we had to feed them porridge twice a day. My dog Tomik was of course outraged and a little disappointed every time he saw his bowl and looked at me with eyes that seemed to say: "Is that all?"

I brought my dad to Tykhon's room, where two grandmothers had settled down. We gave him a laptop so he could relax and watch a movie and not dwell on recent events.

My mother went back to her apartment to pick up her cat, Dymka.

We warned her it was dangerous but she wouldn't listen. She found the cat under the sofa, terrified but alive, hiding amongst the debris of broken glass from shattered windows. Sadly her pet tortoises did not survive. In the heart of winter with no windows they had froze to death. Bonnie and Nosik had lived with her for four years so it was quite the blow. However mum still returned safely with the cat and I closed the cat in my bedroom until the other animals would settle around him.

When I looked at the cupboards I realized we didn't have much essentials, so I decided to try a new store I had heard about when standing in line for food yesterday. So I decided to visit it hoping it may have more food items. When I arrived there was a queue right around the building, which I joined.

I waited two and a half hours. It was very cold and I found myself hopping on the spot to keep warm. I met two women in the line who also owned dogs and they were waiting in line to get them food too as pet shops were closed.

One of the women's son served in the ATO in the east and was demobilized only a year ago. He just started to get used to a peaceful life, found a job, started dating a girl - she lamented.

Her son had gone to the military registration and enlistment office on the very first day and she didn't know where he was now. The military couldn't confirm his location. I felt so sorry for this lady! It was her only son and it was killing her not knowing. She looked on the verge of tears but she didn't cry.

When I finally got into the store, I had no luck – it was the same story as yesterday. There were practically no basic products. I did manage to get a couple of liters of milk, three loaves of bread, rice and pasta, and a frozen liver that had probably been in a freezer for five years. But I also had dogs who wanted at least some meat... When I was at the checkout I saw a woman with a bag of sugar.

– Where did you get sugar? – I asked.

 – Over there! – She replied, – beside the weighing scales.

– What a pity that I did not notice! The children have been asking for sugar.

– Go get some! – Said the man behind me.

– Really? Will you save my spot?

– Of course! Be quick!

I was surprised that people are willing to wait for me to pick up sugar, despite the fact that they were already waiting two and a half hours to get into the store.

And I ran to the end of the store, there was a huge box of sugar, next to which there were about 10 people. In Ukraine we weigh sugar into bags. I took as much as I could and double bagged the sugar. I ran to the scales to weigh and print the price tag . It was 3kgs (6lbs).

(Even writing this now I still feel confusion, haste, nervousness, palpitation that I had felt when I ran around the store with this sugar)

I rejoined the queue for checkouts and when it was my turn to scan the sugar bag burst! Sugar fell all over the floor... I froze, and just stood watching it pour on the floor. I nearly shed tears...

The Cashier took the bag from me and re bagged it. And I still stood in confusion and could not do anything, I was so confused.

– Go and weigh your sugar again, – said the guy from behind me, – we'll wait.

I don't even remember what he looked like, tall or short, fat or thin, but for some reason I still remember his voice. I again ran to the scales, weighed it and very carefully carried this bag to the cash register in an embrace.

I paid, packed everything in my backpack and went home thinking of the kindness of the gentleman behind me.

I came home, put away the groceries, told my family the story about sugar, and climbed into the basement because the siren was howling again.

Recently, there were problems with communication, it was difficult to get through to somewhere, only there was WiFi in the house, the Internet worked, you could watch the news and chat with friends via Viber. But there was no Internet in the shelter, and we sat there listening to distant explosions and did not even know what was happening outside, we just sat until the explosions subsided.

When we got out of the basement and read the news, it turned out that the city center was bombed, the Shchors cinema and the children's clinic were bombed. It was very close to us, about 20 minutes on foot, and by car about three minutes. They also said that the water pipes were damaged and we would have to collect out own water.

Before that, we collected several canisters of rainwater, but now we have collected in all the containers that were available. The men found empty 25 litre bottles, which were in the shed. They were left from the previous owners, most likely wine was aged in them. They could be used to take a bath or something to flush in the toilet.

It was difficult to imagine how much water we would need for 16 people to live normally. But we were optimistic that we would be ok. There was a nearby river so if it got tough we could draw water from there and boil it.

Information also came that the Russians were building a platoon crossing over the river, where the bridges had been blown up but the Ukrainians were defending the river shooting at them. It was all so strange, like something you would see in a film. It was still hard to accept this was reality.

Kostya sent photos of my eldest Tykhon on Viber. In the photo he was cheerful and happy. It was as if they were in some kind of parallel reality. They were safe in the monastery with Christ… Surely, Russians, who are also Orthodox Christians, would not come to a monastery and bomb!

Kostya said that distant explosions were quietly heard somewhere. As it was clear from the news, it was Sumy, the regional center not far from their monastery, that was bombed. Kostya again talked about coming, but again I persuaded him not to risk it.

They prayed every day for peace, this was their main work. He asked what we needed, and I told him about the shops and that the second day I could not take sunflower oil for frying. He did not understand why I was so worried about the products, which you can buy another day. But I talked to the cashiers in the store and they said that there was no food shipments to the city, they only sell what they had stock and storage and didn't know when new food would come.

At one point, Lena's mother called and said that tanks were driving past their house along the main street.

– Whose tanks? –Lena almost screamed. But her mother was not very versed in technology and identification marks, and she herself was obviously very frightened. Tanks moving through the center of the city. This message stunned everyone.

Yura and Vitya, after hearing this news, thought that the Russians had broken through the defenses and entered the city. They began to prepare axes to protect their families in case of emergency. I began to persuade them not to do stupid things, we are civilians. The Russians will not target us!

 Let's hope that they will not come near the estate at all, and if they do, they will come in and have a look around and leave again.

At that time, I could not imagine that the Russian soldiers, whom we always considered brothers, could hurt me and my family.

Yes, they were deceived, they were told some nonsense so that they would go to free someone here, but they don't want to kill us for real – that's what I thought. That's exactly what I thought. Not all people thought so, many have long considered the Russians to be real killers and enemies. Only I didn't believe it.

When someone knocked on the window, everyone was really scared, it seemed that what we were most afraid of had come. Yura and Vitya told me not to look out at all, but I decided to look from the next room who was standing by the window.

Thankfully it was our friends, they had been phoning a lot trying to check on us probably phoning when we were sitting in the basement. Worried they decided to come visit on foot. They did not come in, handed over a loaf of bread and apples, and went on. It was so strange that someone remembered our family and despite the danger came to visit.

In the distance to the north, automatic bursts were heard and it seemed to us that they were getting closer and closer. And it seemed to us that the fighting was already going on in the city. Later we learned that these were our tanks, which were traveling from south to north to where the enemy was coming from and that this was the shortest way.

There were many children in the shelter, and during these three days six kilograms of dirty things had already accumulated. Since I had to save water in my house, we packed up and took it to Yulia in a neighboring house to do laundry while there was a lull. When I went outside to hang out the laundry, I saw that the neighbors on the other side were boarding up the windows.

– Are you going to leave? – I asked.

– Well, no. Where should we go? Here is our home. And the boards are for the blast wave not to knock out the windows.

– We also stay at home. If you need help, call me, – I said.

– Of course. Let's stick together. And call if you need anything.

– Have you enough essentials?

– Yes. Enough for now thankfully. Do you have cigarettes?

– No. We have a smoker suffering here, too.

Lena's husband, Vitya, smoked a pipe and usually bought tobacco from farmers in the market, but for two days now the tobacco had run out, and there was nowhere to get any.

During the next raid, when we went down to the basement and it turned out that my phone was dying, I realized that my charging cable was upstairs, and then I decided to always carry it with me, because it is not known where I will spend the next hour, upstairs or downstairs.

I had a jacket with two zip pockets and I wore that jacket all the time that I lived in the basement. There was always a charger, a phone, a flashlight and house keys inside the jacket.

When I left home and came to England I wore it too. It was a good jacket, but finally it fell apart and had to be thrown away. But it was so dear to me that it lay in the box for some time, I could not put it in a bag.

When everything calmed down, we decided to go for a walk with the dogs to the river. We took all three dogs, I took my children Misha and Nykon, too . I asked if anyone else wanted to come for a walk with the other children but no one wanted to, everyone was afraid. And I was afraid to be afraid, afraid to admit the thought that something would happen to me.

In general, I enjoy walking – it clears the brain. I think this daily escape and fresh air helped me not to panic and have the strength to live. The dogs were running, the children were running nearby, and I ran, waved my arms to warm up. And everything would have seemed as always, if not for the air raid alarm, and we just cheerfully ran home.

We ate again in the basement, squatting. When the alarm ended, the children no longer fell asleep. It was still impossible to turn on the light in the house, so they went to bed downstairs, and I also helped the grandparents to settle down and went to bed too. I began to go to bed earlier, knowing that the bombing would begin early in the morning...

6. The city was surrounded.

Explosions were heard all night. But I no longer got up and ran to the basement, I began to get used to it. A person gets used to everything, it's true.

Despite the shelling from our side, the Russians built a pontoon crossing over the river and went from the other side of the city, completely surrounding it. Of course I still get confused about the dates of main events, but in my opinion, from that day on, we were completely surrounded. That is... it was not possible to leave and enter the city, supplies were no longer delivered either.

I got up around six, my mother was already in the kitchen, life began to become familiar. We drank coffee and figured out what to cook for breakfast.

There was no WIFI or phone lines in the house. It was reported that the Russians jammed our towers and instead of the signal of our telecom operators, they gave their signal. How they managed to do this, I honestly do not know. My mother used to Skype every day with her sister, who lived in Moldova.

However with the line down, it had been days since they kept in touch. My mother knew her sister would be worried so we decided to go over the bridge to try to call her (hopefully there would be signal there). We took Tom with us and left.

It was early morning, the sun was just peeking out in the east. At the intersection of the streets we heard some noise, several male neighbors were visible. We got closer to find out what was going on. And when they came up, they saw that they had caught a burgular – a young guy who was climbing around the yards.

It turned out that our neighbors organized something like a squad and took it in turns to patrol the streets so that there would be no riots, because there were no police in the city.

There were houses people had abandoned and thieves began to appear in the city, who went to these houses and stole valuable things.

I don't know what happened to thieves who were caught by the neighborhood patrols. They just said they would take him somewhere.

In the future, many cases of looting became widespread. And when robbers were caught, they were tied to a post with tape with their pants down to shame them. Such lynching in wartime is a common thing.

Mom and I went over the bridge, and the phone picked up a weak signal. I dialed Aunt Galya, she answered almost immediately, as if she was waiting for our call. Mom picked up the phone and said that everyone is alive and well, there may not be enough time to explain more. Indeed, almost immediately the connection was cut off, and we went back.

When the children began to wake up and crawl out of the basement to wash, it turned out that most of them got sick. Almost everyone had snot and cough. The basement was still damp and cold. I immediately began to think about what to do, I had to decide on my own and quickly.

The simplest and most effective remedy for children's colds is washing with salt and water. A little salt added to the water, washing noses and gargling throats can work wonders.

So my morning was filled with rinsing everyone's nose and making them gargle. Surprisingly, almost no one resisted except for little Katya. Water with salt helps very well in the initial stages, provided that you do it several times a day.

It was important to try every remedy we knew, because if the children got worse at this stage or needed hospital there would be no doctors to help.

A friend Zhenya called, said that I should go to the main street, he would bring me groceries. It was unexpected for me, but I got ready and rode my bike. As it turned out, it was Kostya who called him and asked if they had sunflower oil, he tried to help us with at least something.

Zhenya was also somewhere in the private sector on the outskirts and they still had groceries in the store, he came in and bought me a couple of bottles of sunflower oil and brought me to the center.

I was very glad to see him, I wanted to talk with him longer, but Zhenya was very worried. Along the way, he was stopped several times by patrols, they interrogated, questioned, and even checked his phone to make sure he was not a Russian spy. He said he would get out of town while he still could.

Which he did.... Later he would write us a message where he told us how he escaped with his family. They drove by car to the Desna River, and since there were no bridges, they simply abandoned the car.

They found a boat and crossed to the other side by boat. From there they walked to the Domnica Monastery. At that time, many already understood that Russians surrounded the city and made attempts to leave.

There were many who didn't survive or faced danger and they ran into the Russians while fleeing. Many cars were shot at. It took courage to decide to leave the city.

On my way home, I decided to stop by my store. Driving up, I saw a crowd of people near the entrance to the basement floor, where there was a lamp shop. I drove over to find out what was going on. It turned out that they organized a collection of things and money for the military and people who were left without anything as a result of the bombing.

Every day people brought what they could: sleeping bags, sleeping mats, food, as well as shoes and things.

Of course, I couldn't stay aside! I drove to my own store and collected winter shoes and socks and just brought as many as I could to donate.

A couple of times the thought occurred I would have to pay back the business loan I took out to buy stock and had no way to repay it now as I had nothing left to sell... But I drove them away with one simple answer: if tomorrow a rocket hits my store, then I won't have any money or shoes to sell anyway… and there are people who need it more than me… soldiers in the winter in the trenches and people who have lost everything, their homes and families.

I drove back home, there were a little more people in the streets. People were starting to get used to things too... They didn't have a choice but to adapt to the sirens and explosions.

I went to the pharmacy hoping to buy medicine for the children, but all the pharmacies were closed, and in one that was open, there was nothing anti-inflammatory that could help. There was no medication so it meant once again I would just have to use salt and water to help the children and I went home with the intention of washing the noses of the children again.

Since the connection was gone, only the Internet remained. But this morning, the Internet in my house also disappeared, apparently the line was damaged. But Yura had another Internet operator, which was still operating. And so Yura boosted the Internet signal from his house and installed a WiFi router in the shelter. It turned out to be a very interesting situation, if you wanted to talk to someone on Viber or watch the news, you had to go down to the shelter. But at least now, during the air raid alerts, you could sit on the phone and so the time passed faster.

After lunch they bombed heavily on the outskirts from the north. The explosions were very loud, when I went down to the basement, the cat Shadow followed me, he didn't like all this either, and he felt calmer with people. But Tom did not want to go down, although he was very worried. He always ran near the hatch and wagged his tail.

It was already becoming a tradition that when we descended, I took a prayer book and read Psalm 90 aloud. The rector of the monastery where Kostya was, said that if we read this psalm, our house would survive. And since it's the only thing we could do, we did it. We prayed knowing that we could not influence the situation in any way, we could only hope for God's protection.

When the alarm passed and we went out into the yard, there were huge clouds of smoke in the north, as it turned out later, a building materials supermarket had been blown up, a very large store on the outskirts of the city. The store was on fire, and therefore there was a lot of smoke, which was clearly visible from anywhere in the city.

Aunt Tanya was very worried about her apartment, which was located in the northern part of the city. She was going to go see if everything was all right. We persuaded her not to do this, because it is very dangerous. My mother went to her apartment only because there was a cat and the apartment was on the other side. Going in the direction from which the enemy seemed to be approaching was a bad idea and what was there to see?

 But in order to calm Aunt Tanya a little, we went with her across the bridge and called a neighbor. The neighbor said that the apartment is intact, the glass is intact, at least for today. And Aunt Tanya calmed down a little.

Yura's boss called and said that he needed to go to work. Yulia was very frightened and begged Yura not to go anywhere, but he said that he had to, he could not stay.

She continued to persuade him, saying that the Russians were about to come, and he replied: well, let them try to meet him.

Then I decided to intervene, showed him the children and said thst right now they need their father alive and not six feet underground. The enemy should be dealt with by professional soldiers, not by civilians with an axe for a machine gun. The children didn't need another fallen hero, they needed him alive, and I told him to drop his youthful maximalism and think with his head.

I showed him where the key to the gate was hidden, if he suddenly needed to return urgently and asked if he saw the Russians not to be a hero, but to run home through the backyards, then we would decide what to do. We stood with them in front of the icon and prayed.

Julia collected food for him for the day, and he went, and we stayed. Yulia looked devastated, she didn't say anything, but it was clear that she had a hole in her soul and really wanted to cry, but she probably couldn't afford it so as not to scare the children.

Yes, the pork liver that I got for the dogs in the store turned out to be of quite decent quality. And we prepared it for both people and dogs. The dogs, of course, were delighted, even Tom ate everything and asked for more. The cats also ate porridge with liver, no one was picky. Even Aunt Tanya's cat Milka ate porridge, which Aunt Tanya was very surprised at. But my mother's cat Dymka still didn't eat porridge, well, let her wait, gets hungry – will eat. We found ourselves so grateful to have food – we are not starving, thank God!

Of course, we did still have challenges. We were still unfamiliar with one another's habits. Naturally, sometimes there were conflicts in simple everyday things. Lena practically did not participate in cooking and washing dishes, and this began to annoy some people.

Galya began to tell me:

– Tell her to clean up after herself, so that she participates in cooking. We cannot be constantly feeding her children and washing the dishes for them.

I said:

– I think that Lena is an adult and understands everything, if she has the strength, then she will help anyway.

But I decided to say a few words to Lena, because she had five in her family and it was hard to cook and clean for them when they were unwilling to lend a hand.

But when I pulled Lena about this, she answered with irritation:

– Just leave our dishes in the sink, I will wash them later, just stay out of my business.

Of course, I didn't like this answer either, I don't recall saying anything offensive, I just expressed the opinion of the majority so that she herself would decide how to modify her behavior. Resentment ran between us. I just walked away and went about my business.

We are best friends, and had been friends for 15 years, and of course during that time we had had small arguments… But when we did usually we would go home and two days later we would met, apologized and continued communication.

But now I had no place to go and no time to waste. Anything could happen: tonight we could be bombed or attacked and life was too short to stay angry with friends. So instead I just went up and hugged her:

– Forgive me, I'm probably just tired.

– And you forgive me, – Lena said, – I'll try to do more to help!
– Oh, it's not that important! Do what you can.

I understand that not everyone has the strength when it is needed, sometimes in a stressful situation there is not enough moral strength to lift themselves up and to do something. It's good that God endowed me with moral strength so that I could keep order in the house and go for groceries. We each went about our business and never returned to this problem.

Since the children were sick, I decided to leave them to sleep upstairs. At least the ones I was responsible for. But just in case, I called Anna and asked if her child could be left upstairs for the night and not in a shelter.

I was scared that if something happened to Misha at night Anna would not forgive me for this, so I decided to share the responsibility with her. Anna stayed in the south of Kyiv, where she came to work. They, of course, did not work, but simply the whole team sat in place without being able to leave.

From her work, there was no way to get to Kyiv. When she called a taxi, she was told it could be thousands to bring her to Kyiv, although the distance was only 10 km. She just didn't have that amount of money. And even if she had reached Kyiv, there would be no transport to Chernihiv, and she would have been stuck there.

They hadn't been bombed yet, there were air raid alerts from time to time, but it was quiet. Maybe that's why she easily agreed that if I think it's better, then let Misha sleep upstairs. How could I know which is better? Misha was glad to go to bed upstairs, he did not understand how dangerous it really was. It was I who had seen enough of the news and understood what was happening during the shelling of houses. I put Nykon on the bed with me. I didn't undress either, so that if the bombing was close, I would immediately run to the shelter. It was a very restless night. I hardly slept, listening to the shots, about to carry the child to the basement.

I lay, listened to the shots and thought about how I would act if the windows were to fly out now and pulled a blanket over Nykon's head. Then I thought, if suddenly there was an explosion inside the house and there was a fire, then how I would jump through the window, but there were mosquito nets on the windows, they would need to be squeezed out. And what if my legs are torn off what could I use as a tourniquet? These thoughts haunted my night and sleep was impossible... Machine gun bursts were heard in the distance and I expected that now the shots would be closer and I would carry Nikon down. And then it seemed to me that the gate was opening and Yura was returning home, but he was still not there and there was no contact with him...

7. We clog windows

I didn't sleep at all, of course. There was shelling at 4 am, I decided to take Nykon to the basement. I also woke Misha up and took him to the basement.

The frequency and strength of the bombing increased every day. Previously the rockets came only from the north, now they rained down from all sides. On the outskirts, where there were private, one-story houses, there was already a lot of destruction. When the shelling ended, my mother and I sat down to drink morning coffee and make plans.

– We need to go and board up the windows in the flat,– Mom said. – It's winter and with the frost, furniture and things will deteriorate.

– Yes. – Mom Galya joined. – and remove the glass from the entrance, otherwise the neighbors will think that we are lazy.

– What neighbors? You don't think anyone lives there, do you? The water and heating were turned off so that the pipes would not burst. Who would sit there in an empty cold stone box?

– Well, you think what you want, but you need to go clean up and the neighbor from the second floor asked to clean up her apartment.

– Lord have mercy! Are you out of your mind, or what? They are bombing the city center! You're planning to run there to clean up glass? – I was at a loss. How can you even think about some furniture and things when it can all be purchased again. The only thing you can't buy is your life and health!

But they were both adamant to return and repair damage so I gave up debating.

– Okay. Now I'll pack my things and let's go.

I found rolls of plastic bags in the warehouse. How long they had been there and what for, I didn't know. I was just very glad that I didn't have time to throw them away before.

I had meant to clear out the warehouse ages ago and throw out all the junk left by the previous owners but I never found the time for a deep clean. Which turned out to be a small blessing. I now found so many useful items for DIY there, when the hardware stores had closed, including planks, which would be useful to secure the bags over damaged windows.

Before we started repairs we had a quick bite to eat and walked along the main street towards my parents' home, me and three grandmothers with plastic bags and planks in our hands.

When we approached the last crossroads, the air raid alarm howled. We were stopped by the military at the checkpoint:

– Where are you going? Quickly! Hurry to shelter!

– Yes, we're going home. – I answered. The military man looked at me like I was crazy: – You need to go to the shelter. Now!

The shelter that the military man pointed to was under a multi-storey building, and it seemed to me more dangerous than returning to our house. So we ran back home, explosions were heard somewhere far away, but we got back without incident.

Yura returned home from work, said that valuable things and documentation were taken out of the offices, because looters could have taken them. That's what they'd been doing all night.

At breakfast, I once again tried to dissuade the grandmothers from cleaning up the flat, but they were adamant:

– We will go the other way – past the hospital, there should not be military men there, – they said.

I didn't want to go where the military did not advise to go at all, but I couldn't let them go by themselves.

The children woke up, I washed everyone's nose again and made them gargle salt as they were still ill and we couldn't access pharmacy medicine. I took Nykon and Misha with me to run with the dogs. I made them run with all their might and cough – so that the mucus from the throat and lungs would go away. Such was my use of medieval medicine.

When we returned and had breakfast, we again got ready to make our way to the neighboring area to the apartments of our parents, on foot. It took 20-25 minutes to walk along a straight road, but we went around roadblocks, courtyards, and the road eventually took us forty five minutes. We walked through the hospital and saw ordinary private cars with red crosses painted on them. As I understood, there were not enough ambulances, and people organized private cars to bring the wounded from the outskirts of the city. In front of us, an elderly man with a wounded leg was taken out of the car, he groaned heavily, it was clear that he was in pain. We went further, because we had our own goal.

As we wandered through the streets near my parents' old home, it was heartbreaking to see the damage. Windows were broken in many houses around. Basically, old wooden Soviet frames could not stand the shock from bombs, in some places the glass was intact, where there were new modern windows. But there were a lot of old windows and all the asphalt was strewn with splinters. It's good that we left the dogs at home, they could cut their paws walking along the streets. And now it was dangerous to ride a bicycle here, if the tire got punctured, you would be left without a bicycle as there are no shops open to buy repair kits.

When we approached our parents' house, we saw the extent of the destruction. It turned out that the rocket did not even hit the house, but nearby, 10 meters from the house, there was a large funnel 3 meters wide and 1.5 meters deep. Only a piece of shrapnel hit the house, and because of it there was a fire. The entire entrance burned out, it's good that the fire did not spread to the second storey of the house.

At the main entrance the windows had flown out, we climbed the glass. Mom Galya and Aunt Tanya went to the apartment of her husband's parents, and my mother and I went to her apartment. Mom had a small apartment, only one room and a kitchen. And everything was strewn with glass. I decided that we would not tidy up, but only nail bags to the windows. I took a hammer, climbed onto the windowsill, and then it began...

First, the siren howled, and it became scary, very scary. I was standing on the windowsill on the forth floor, by the broken window with a hammer in my hands and nails in my teeth. Very quickly I began to command my mother to give the planks and the bags. I think that we boarded up the window in the room in 5-10 minutes, I did everything so quickly.

But when I was about to go to the kitchen, a plane flew over our house... The house shook!

I pushed my mother to the doorway, they say there you can be saved if the house collapses. Mom and I stood in the aisle between the room and the corridor, and prayed until the house stopped moving from side to side.

But the work was not finished and we continued with haste.

– Come on, faster! – I said to my mother and we ran to the kitchen window. The hammer in my hands was trembling, but I tried to do everything carefully so as not to hit my finger, because then I would not be able to hold the hammer. I did everything very quickly, and we ran out of the apartment. I ran into the apartment next door.

– Ready? – I asked mother Galya.

 – We've just removed the glass, – she replied.

I wanted to scream and stomp my feet: how can you clean up something when planes are flying overhead? We came with one goal: to close the windows with cellophane! Fortunately, Kostya's parents had all the double-glazed windows replaced with new ones, except for the kitchen.

– Let's hammer! – I said, climbing onto the windowsill and trying on cellophane.

– Stop! – said mother Galya, giving me a hammer. – Why are you trying on such an ugly patterned bag? I have a beautiful one!

And with these words she brought a piece of green and crimson bag. I cannot convey in literary words what it wanted to break from my lips.

But I suppressed my irritation and began to nail the beautiful one, there was no time for arguments, because explosions were heard very close and the house began to stagger again.

– Run! – I screamed flying off the windowsill after hammering the last nail. We ran along the porch, the house staggered and it seemed that it was about to collapse.

– Wait! – Mother Galya screamed. – I opened the apartment of my neighbor from the second floor and I can't get the key out!

I stopped and froze for a few seconds. It seemed to me that my heart would jump out of my chest.

– Where?

– Here! – she said, pointing to the door, we just ran to the second floor. I looked at the key in the door, my mind going over my options. If it doesn't get out now, then we'll leave it like that, I was not going to lose my life because of the neighbor's property.

– God Bless! – I said, took the key, moved it a little, found the moment when it clung to the lock and turned it twice. I took it out, gave it to my mother Galya and without a word ran downstairs, the grandmothers hurried after me.

We ran out of the entrance and went down to the basement, there were about fifteen people who continued to live in the house. People continued to live in a house without heating and water, because they simply had nowhere to go. In the same place, sat two children of 5-8 years. They sat doomedly and fiddled with their toys in their hands, and my mother covered them with a blanket brought from home. It was just a basement, and if a rocket had hit the house, we would have simply been buried alive under the house.

But after a while the explosions stopped, the house stopped shaking, and we went home.

Already at home, we learned that several houses had been blown up not far from us, in the Hradetsky district. People got hurt. There was a video on the network of how the grandmother was lying, saying something to herself, and her legs were broken and blood was flowing. And later we learned that she died from blood loss. I'm just crazy about the situation, how can you stand and film a person bleeding? What's wrong with you, people! Therefore, I have few photos and videos, most of the time it was not at all up to it.

When we walked back, we saw the guys who were tearing off the signs with the names of the streets. The idea was that the Russian tanks would get lost when they entered the city. Personally, such measures in the age of the Internet and Google maps seemed like nonsense to me. I even got angry with them: I pay taxes, they buy signs on them, but they have nothing to do but to tear them down. I don't know if my thoughts are politically correct but do not view them unkindly. Perhaps it was from the transferred horror that anger came out.

We also met a friend who was in camouflage and with a machine gun, he also went to defend his city. I told him:

– Take care of yourself!

And I thought to myself: where are you going? You have two small children! If the Russians come, they will sweep away the whole city and you along with it. And what can you do against them, with the machine gun in your hand which you had picked up only a week before!

This is how stress comes out, in irritation and condemnation. At that time, I still did not believe that it would be for a long time, our presidents sat down for negotiations, and it seemed to me that now everything would end, and the signs would be torn down and children would live without fathers.

We came home, ate something and we did not have time to wash the dishes, as another alarm drove us into the bomb shelter.

While we were sitting, we shared our impressions about the clogging of windows and how a high-rise building staggers when a jet plane flies over it. Little Dima wanted to go to the toilet, and Yulia put him on the potty. He did his business, but the smell began to spread in the small room, and the bombing was very heavy, and it was dangerous to leave the shelter.

There were a lot of jars for preserving cucumbers and jam in the basement. We canned what Dima had made. In some areas of Chernigov, people could not leave the bomb shelter for several days, and I think they also preserved the waste. Just imagine that you need to go to the toilet, but there is none...

When everything was quiet outside, we climbed out to the top. The sun was setting, it was quiet. I again took the children and my mother to run with the dogs. And she herself ran and tried to breathe deeply and clear her throat, it became warmer in the basement, but dampness remained, and there was a fungus on the wall, we knew it could make us sick. We decided to remove the fungus from the walls if possible. Lena put on a respirator, and began to remove the top layer of whitewash with a shovel, and Yulia and I took out all the things. Vitya and Yura got out and knocked out the mattresses.

When we got all the things from the shelter, we found a bag with food that Lena had taken from home, of course, it all got spoilt. She dropped it down there on the first day, in case she had to stay in a bomb shelter all the time and forgot. The products were necessary, but nothing could be done with the ones in the bag, I had to throw them away.

Most of the windows in the house were already sealed with cardboard, and the lights could be turned on. Children ran around the house and made noise quite carelessly, as if there had never been a war. Someone was drawing, Nykon began to make crafts, Katya hid in the closet and played with Rada, and Roma pulled out Tykhon's Lego. If Tykhon found out that some other children were touching his Lego, he would certainly be indignant, but now he was not there, and I didn't tell Roma anything, let him play. In fact, no one knows what will happen next and what will happen to the house and to us.

A neighbor knocked on the window, he lived not far from us, brought a 12-liter can of milk. The cows continued to give milk and continued to be milked, but the market did not work and neighboring farmers simply brought it to the city, and there it was taken by volunteers and taken to the shelters where there are children. So the neighbor took us on, knowing that we had seven children. No one took any money, the product should not be wasted anyway.

Later, we highlighted in the news that shells had hit some farm. There was a video with dead cows, I felt sorry for them. Children in Ukraine grow up on milk, drink it every day. So that the milk would not disappear for several days, we boiled it and took it to the barn in the cold. The children were very happy, they missed milk.

Since after the next raid some power lines were damaged, the air raid alarm, the siren did not turn on. We realized that the alarm was when we already heard the sounds of the bombing. Children without command poured into the cellar, we followed them. While we were sitting in the cellar, we checked the news on the Internet and a message came that one of our friends had died defending our city. Lena burst into tears, saying:

– How come? Why? What for?

And I just sat there and thought that this was just the beginning and there would be more dead friends

Nobody needs this stupid war, why has this been going on for days?

Why can't the heads of our states come to an agreement so that our cities don't get destroyed, our people don't die? When my children swear and fight, I tell them: do you want to be right or happy? And they answer:

– Happy!

– Then stop proving yourself right, make peace, play happily.

Why can't presidents do this?

When the explosions subsided, Vitya and I went outside to listen to whether everything was quiet and whether it was possible to leave the shelter. It was already dark, and since there was a blackout throughout the city, neither streetlights nor traffic lights worked, no lights were on in anyone's windows, the stars were very clearly visible. I have not looked at the stars for a long time, they are hard to see in the city, but here there was such beauty. We began to look at them, remembering the constellations. It turned out that Vitya knew a lot of constellations and showed me new ones.

Thus ended another day in the occupation, a day of pain and fear and hope that it would all end tomorrow. But every day it only got worse...

8. Crackers

The morning started with exposions. The sirens stopped hauling, but the explosions were deafening by dawn. I got up, pulled on my socks and a sweater, the rest of the clothes were on me anyway, and went to the kitchen. I looked into the basement, everyone was sleeping there, I didn't go down, because although there were explosions, I could hear that it was far from us.

The Grandmothers were already sitting in the kitchen discussing what to cook for dinner. Honestly, what would the world do without Grandmothers, always prepared for anything?

There were also rumors that a large supermarket would open nearby, in the basement of the local shopping center. It was very large, and it would be nice to visit there. Perhaps food would be brought there and stored, it was underground after all.

Mom and I decided to go there together to purchase more food. Its more fun shopping together. And both grandmother Galya and grandmother Tanya were going to go to grandmother Tanya's apartment.

I criticized their idea and ordered them not to go anywhere because it was dangerous. If a construction supermarket was blown up, and Tanya's grandmother's apartment was just in that direction, then it is not clear where the bombs will fall today. They sighed, but stopped arguing.

Vitya crawled out of the basement, angry and gloomy, grumbling something and making tea for himself.

– Why are you so gloomy? – I asked.

– I want to smoke! It's my third day without tobacco, I don't know how much longer I can take it! – Vitya exclaimed and turned back to tea.

– Yes, I understand. We will go to the store today, if there is any tobacco, I'll get it while I'm there.

Then mother Galya got up, went into the room where they slept and brought a bag of tobacco into the kitchen and handed it to Vitya.

– Where?! Where were you able to get it?

– Where did I get it? – Mom Galya answered with humor. – Doesn't matter as it's not there anymore.

Vitya almost jumped into the street to fill his pipe. I assumed that Galya's mother had tobacco at home, and when we boarded up the windows, she probably took it with her, and then she probably forgot to give it to Vitya.

Where did she get the tobacco from? Maybe from her youngest son? He smoked a lot, then again, he lived and worked in Odessa for years and wouldn't have time to visit. Again I was amazed by how incredible Grandmothers were – they always know everything and are prepared.

My mother and I grabbed backpacks and went to the large store, which was located on the basement floor of the shopping center. We got to the entrance of the mall around 8 am and there was already a queue. We stood in the cold until nine, and then they opened the doors and let us inside the shopping center, but the doors of the store were still closed until 10. The door to the store was opened by the military with machine guns, I sensed they were worried that there may be disorder and chaos with people fighting for essentials.

They were tense, perhaps there had been trouble previously in the store. While we were queuing the bombing began. We heard the explosions very faintly downstairs, but it was very scary. All the people were standing and looking around, someone turned around and walked away from the mall, because if the shell had hit there, then we could just be buried alive. But everything worked out and at 10:00 the doors of the store were open. People poured in in a continuous stream, no one detained people, since the store was large and could accommodate everyone. Mom and I took a trolley and went around the store, or rather ran round. I remember that we found salt in bags. We lifted a few kilograms, because my salt was running out at home, and it's hard to eat bland food.

We grabbed some frozen fish which was questionably edible and bread! We were thrilled to see bread. There was plenty here and we grabbed ten loaves to celebrate as it had been hard to live without bread. It didn't look great! It was grey, half the weight of a regular loaf and twice the price, but we didn't care – we happily stocked up. With inflation in the country, with the war and food prices rising rapidly, everyone had to stockpile essentials.

No alcohol was sold and the off-sales was closed which was probably for the best. There was enough trouble in the city without police having to deal with drunken showdowns. Nor was there anything to celebrate, drink and be merry.

When we returned home, it turned out that Tanya and Galya had snuck out to grandmother Tanya's apartment despite my warnings not to go!

Oh, well! They were back safe and I couldn't control them as they were independent adults. In hindsight it became clear to me why earlier they immediately fell silent when I told them not to go anywhere, they decided not to argue and   do their own thing when I was out.

Oksana and Kostya, good friends of ours, came to us riding their bicycles. In peacetime, they baked cakes, gingerbread and other sweets. They made it to order and sold it on the market. They brought us an apple pie, went into the house for ten minutes, asked how we were doing, told us how they were managing. When the war began, many people left, and in the city there were many old and disabled people who now had no one to help.

Some of them hadn't left their apartments for several years, social workers came to them and brought food. And without help now they could just starve to death. Oksana and Kostya, having heard this news, could not remain indifferent to their suffering and began to cook food and deliver it to old people around the city. They started from their home, then switched to the local area, and now they traveled around various areas. They cooked potato soup, even cutlets.

Amazing people. Their generosity was incredible. Nobody asked them to do this, nobody made them do it and nobody paid them either and yet these incredible people did it! Having only a pedal bike at theor disposal they stood in line in stores to buy food, brought it home, cooked it and then went around the old people and fed them. I later learned about some more friends who also helped the elderly and disabled people.

When they left, I decided to go for a walk with the dogs, take Misha and Nykon with me and maybe run. I tried to pursuade Lena to join us.

– Come out with us! You will go crazy in this dungeon! And the children need some air.

– What if they start bombing?

– They'll start bombing, we'll run back.

And she agreed. She dressed the children, dressed herself, and we went to the river. We ran around the overgrown football field with dogs, played with children, laughed and joked. It did us the world of good! Getting out in the air was thrilling and we couldn't stop smiling. The dogs were the happiest of all, their owners were with them every day. The weather was fine, and while we were walking it was quiet, so I suggested to Lena we drop the kids back and go for a proper hike.

We returned home, left the children who were worn out by their excursion at this point, took Vitya and went towards the city center. It was so good, we crossed the bridge, and began to enter the neighboring quarter, when suddenly a shell exploded somewhere nearby.

And then the second and the third!

The blast made the houses tremble and the windows tinkle. We were between two nine-story buildings. We were terrified that the buildings might now collapse.

There were few people on the street, maybe two or three people on the neighboring side, who ran in terror. We, too, sprinted as fast as we could home bound. Lena was very frightened after this incident. I knew it wouldn't be possible to convince her to go for a walk anytime soon, she was very shook and happy to stay safe in the shelter.

As for me, I think I would go crazy trapped in a basement all day, I'm much better in the sun (even if I am dodging shots).

We returned home, climbed into the basement, and grandmothers Galya and Tanya were already sitting there.

– Why didn't you listen to me? I asked you not to go anywhere, – I snapped at them.

– Well, we are not kids and we were fine! We came home safe!

– What if something happened? There is no phone signal here! If you hadn't returned before nightfall what should I do? Get on a bike and look for you! What if something happened to me? And the children would be orphans? You only think of yourselves!

– You shouldn't come looking for us if we disappeared! We were fine anyway!

– How was I supposed to know you were fine? The fact of the matter is that you didn't say anything, packed up and left. Let's be sensible, please!

I felt responsible for everyone who lived in my house, and I really would have gone to look for them if they had not returned before evening. Outside, the explosions did not subside, and we tried to distract ourselves by telling each other about our lives. Yulia and I were still little acquainted, because we had recently moved. And so, we told each other our lives, she told me, and I told her a lot of different stories, life is an interesting thing.

Yura complained that his hair had grown a lot, it was ugly and uncomfortable.

– I have hair trimmers, I can cut the children's hair, – I said.

– Can you cut my hair?

– I can. Can't promise it will look good but if I mess up it can grow back.

– Great, I don't need a model hairstyle here, cut it the best you can.

I looked at Nykon, his hair had grown a lot too. I washed my hair quickly in the basin. Naturally, I didn't wash my child's hair at all, and now it was already dirty, greasy and my hair was long.

– Come on, Nykon, I'll probably cut your hair, then it will grow back.

– And mine. – Dad said. – I also want to be handsome.

– Well, then I should shorten the length, – my mother said, – otherwise it is inconvenient to braid.

When the explosions stopped, and we were convinced that it was quiet outside, I put a stool in the hallway in the only place where I could turn on the light, and in turn I cut all the men's hair and gave my mum a trim. Nykon looked very unusual with short hair, and continuously asked when it would grow back. The next time I cut it was four months later in England, only then did the hair grow back.

Friends came again, brought three loaves of bread. In total, with ours, we got thirteen loaves. Which is of course good, because for sixteen people you need a lot of it. But there was a possibility that we would bin it accidentally as it was stored in a big black bag.

We began to think of ways to preserve or best use the bread, and dad suggested drying the crackers. Great idea considering our situation. Dad cut the bread into thin slices, spread it on a baking sheet and put it in the oven with a small fire. Left the oven door ajar to allow moisture to escape. Each batch dried for about two hours. In a couple of days, dad processed a bag of bread into a bag of crackers. Very cool thing turned out to be these crackers. I could take them with me on the road when I made forays into the city. They could be given to children when they just wanted to have a snack. They could just be thrown out into the yard to the dogs, they also crunched them with pleasure. When I left, I also took a bag of crackers with me. Even when I was already safe and with enough food, I didn't throw out a single cracker, I ate them all because they were dear to me.

There was no telephone connection at all. It was possible to use only the Internet, which Yura installed in the shelter. A sister from Russia again contacted me via the Internet. I told her how we lived, what we ate. She asked me what was really going on with us. I answered that they were bombing around the clock, many districts of Chernigov were destroyed, the house of my parents was destroyed. Products were not delivered to the city, we were surrounded. She said that they only show positive news on their TV channels, that the special operation is going well, there are no casualties among the civilian population, and the like. Nothing is shown about Chernihiv at all, as if there were no hostilities there.

– Well, the Russian troops really just went past Chernihiv and went to Kyiv, but since they are shooting at them from Chernihiv, they shoot back and it turns out that we are being bombed from all sides.

Almost nothing was reported about Chernihiv and according to our news, and we did not understand why. The whole city is being bombed non-stop, I had thoughts that they do not mention Chernihiv because they want to give up the city, or maybe they have already surrendered, the Russians just decided not to enter it. But those were just my thoughts, what really happened, we didn't know. Our troops are now focused on the defense of Kyiv. There were reports on the Internet about free trains from Kyiv to the west, about thousands of people cramming into the trains so that you can't get through to leave. But then I didn't even think about leaving, after a week of the war I was still waiting for a peaceful resolution.

When I went to bed, I felt how strongly my legs were aching. Every day I rode a dozen kilometers on a bicycle to find some food in stores. Most of the shops were closed, and those that were open, there was almost nothing there. Today, for example, I drove through several stores to find batteries for a flashlight, because it was impossible to turn on the light, but sometimes it was necessary to consider at least something. I did not find new batteries and flashlights either.

I wanted to read a book with a flashlight, took it, held it in my hands and put it aside, I just didn't have the energy for it...

9. Grandmothers got sick

Once again, bombs were my alarm clock, but I didn't care anymore. We felt numbness and indifference to it all. We did not live our lives anymore, we just did the necessary things to survive. We sourced food, cooked a meal from whatever we found, fed the children. Every day this was my mission. I had to get up and get essentials so we could survive.

I got up, went to the kitchen, removed the blackout from the small window and let sunlight inside. I turned on the boiler for heating. I did the usual morning chores, cleaning and tidying as expected but at this stage it was almost mechanical. I felt dead inside.

Mom woke up:

– I've been coughing all night, I'm probably getting sick.

– Have you fever?

– No.

– I'll try to get us medicine, gargle your throat with some salt water for now.

I checked the first aid kit. There were some fever powders and a few paracetamol tablets and that was it. *Hardly anything!* I thought: "Well, it's enough for three days to be taken in the morning and evening, maybe this will be sufficient for her…"

Just as I was thinking this, mother Galya came out, sneezing from a cold.

– What's wrong with you?

– Everything is fine. Just a cold. I will drink tea and be fine again, – she answered positively (as always).

– Great, just let's just get you some lemsips too! – I answered just as cheerfully. Only I didn't feel at all cheerful when Aunt Tanya came into the kitchen with a cough.

– Really? The children have recovered from their illness and now it is the grandparents' turn to get sick!

Fate was playing a cruel trick! Could they not somehow take turns!

But it was not a laughing matter. We had almost no medicine in the first aid kit, only enough for emergencies. If they had a fever in the evening there was something there to bring the fever down, but there was little else we could do. We couldn't go to pharmacies. They were empty now.

I tried not to dwell too much on this and focus on the present. For now we had medicine and I gave them all medicine and instructions to wash their noses and gargle their throats with salt water. I also felt a pang thinking of people struggling for medicine: diabetics and cancer patients.

In the morning we got lucky, Kostya's calls briefly got through the communication blockage from the tower. It was such a relief to hear from him!

– Finally, I got through to you, I was going out of my mind with worry! I thought that the house had been blown up and that I had to go and find you!

– Well, what could you do? There is no entry or exit to the city, we are surrounded. How would you, a man of military age, cross the front line? You would be killed by either our men or the others as a spy but let's not talk of these things! How is our son?

– Good. He plays with the other children here. A lot of people came to the Monastery from Sumy and Mariupol. As in ancient times, people seek salvation from the war in the monastery. People come and come, the abbot tries to accomodate them all and give labor according to their abilities. A mother arrived with three daughters from Mariupol, Tykhon has become good friends with them. How are you?

– Well, it depends. Today grandmothers decided to get sick.

– Virus or cold?

– How should I know? I'm not a doctor. For now, just in case it spreads I asked them to be in quarantine. If it is a virus, then it can infect other adults and children, it will be a disaster! Especially since we don't have medicine, but for now they are fine. I recorded some films on the TV and they are resting and watching them now.

– Make sure they rinse their throats with salt and iodine, drink tea with lemon. I wish I could help them more!

– You are an amazing person! But there is nothing you can do to help. Of course, they gargle their throats with salt and drink tea, but there is no lemon. Oh! Thanks for reminding me, I'll be in the store today, I'll try to buy a lemon. I hope you are praying for us there!

– It's the same here really! We have little food too and everyday we are fed here with monastic porridge from various cereals.

– Hardly the same! So far we are not starving. Every day I ride around the city looking for open stores and see what they have. Sometimes I manage to take something. If there is rice I will snap it up! We managed to get 3 kg of pasta, but it was indigestible. Your mother somehow got some Artek porridge, so the dogs ate it with pleasure, but they stopped selling it, and they can't find more. A backpack was brought from my mother's apartment, it's good that we have it.

– What do you think about Nykon's birthday?

– I ordered a T-shirt for him with a picture of a snake, he was born in the year of the snake. A beautiful T-shirt with a bright snake with the inscription Nykon Snake, I need to phone to pick it up. Thanks for reminding me.

When we finished talking, I tried to call and write to the place where I had ordered the T-shirt for Nykon, but there was no answer. They gave us the T-shirt later, when I was already in England, my husband took it and sent it to me. Nykon received his gift with a delay of almost four months, but he was very pleased.

Thinking about my next move, I went to the hall where there was a quarantine for grandmothers. They watched movies and seemed to feel pretty good. When the next shelling began, I really did not want to go down. We were already tired, and we didn't care whether the bomb fell or not. The grandmothers said that they would continue to lie in the hall, because there was not enough space in the shelter, there were children there, and they could get infected. I said that I wouldn't go anywhere either and lay down on one of the mattresses laid out on the floor for the settlers. The explosions became more and more audible, Tom ran into the room and, seeing me on the mattress, began to lie down on my head, as if covering me. It was so unexpected and so sweet. My kind, faithful dog. He was ready to protect me. I miss him very much, I hope to see him again.

When the explosions stopped, I got up and went to get ready for another shopping trip. It was necessary to scout pharmacies for medicines. There were many of them in the area, but we didn't know which shops were still dispensing medicine. I got on my bike and traveled towards the center, but near the bridge I met a neighbor with two bags of flour.

– Flour! Where did you get it?

The neighbor only smiled, mumbled and waved his arms. He was mute, I don't know for what reason, but he was a very open and sympathetic person. He began to wave his hands in the direction of the Hradetsky Hotel.

- To "Hradetsky"? – I asked and he nodded in response.

 – Which store?

He began to poke at the bag in his hands, it had the ATB store logo on it.

– ATB?

– Ay, ay! – he nodded his head.

I got on my bike and rushed towards Hradetsky, where several houses had been bombed recently.

When I arrived at the store, a large number of people was already standing there, it was clear that the information that flour was brought in was spreading very quickly in the besieged city.

I got in line and waited. About an hour later we heard a rumble in the air, and then a jet fighter flew right over us, and maybe it seemed to me, or maybe really there was a wave of air which washed over us.

The plane flew further through the city and it seemed to me that it fired rockets or bombs there because explosions were heard. A whisper was heard in the queue, but no one left, people only pressed closer to the wall near the store. I opened the prayer book on my phone and just began to read the 90th psalm.

God is merciful, and an hour later my turn came to enter the store. I immediately ran into the cereal department, it was empty, but below there were three bags of flour, five kilograms each. I took two of them, I have a lot of people and children at home. I also wanted to pick up the third one, but I decided that perhaps someone further in line also really wants flour.

There were also some cheap canned kinds of meat – chicken stew and pork stew – I took them too. Then when we opened them, their contents looked like dog food, but you could eat them.

I looked for apples and lemons, but there was none of that. I don't remember if I found anything else that day, but I remember flour very vividly. Flour means pancakes for children for breakfast, homemade bread if you need it. Loaded with this stuff, I got back on my bike and rode home.

When I was riding home at the crossroads, I saw an armored personnel carrier at the checkpoint. He was such a handsome newcomer, he probably hadn't been in battle yet. I really wanted to photograph him and show Tykhon, he was very fond of military equipment and weapons. But I restrained myself, there were soldiers at the checkpoint, and it was dangerous. The fact is that everywhere there was a message that they were looking for Russian spies and those who help the Russians.

The suspects were detained on the street, taken from their homes. Maybe these are the right measures during the war, but for some reason I had a rejection of these measures. I just know the history of our country a hundred years ago, when the communists were looking for those who supported tsarism and a lot of innocent people suffered, just because the neighbor did not like them.

I think a certain number of innocent people also suffered in this situation. I hope that they were just scared and in fact the SBU sorted everything out and they were released, I hope there were no lynchings without trial and investigation.

I returned home a winner with 10 kg of flour. Everyone in the shelter appreciated the prey, everyone was delighted. The only thing that upset me was that I did not go to pharmacies. And now it was already evening and it was unlikely we would find one.

So as usual we went for a walk with the dogs. The small river not far from our house was full of ducks. In peacetime, people fed them, I don't know what they ate now, but the wild ones probably found something. The dogs ran and had fun, they were just happy.

As we were returning home, the neighbor's black dog, which considered itself the main one on the street, attacked Caesar (my father's dog). I assumed that Caesar would be stronger, but dad had a tight hold on his leash, so the black dog could hook him. He tore his lip, grabbed a death grip. Even the dog's approaching owner could barely take his pet away.

Misha was very frightened, he was very attached to Caesar. I reassured him:

– Do not be afraid, there is an expression "it will heal like a dog", everything heals quickly with them.

They came home, grandmother Galya took zelenka (aniline dye), anointed Caesar's lip. For some reason, he behaved absolutely calmly, as if it was a common thing for him.

During the next shelling, the power line of our region was damaged, and our light went out. There was no electricity in the whole house, or rather in the entire area. The router was also powered by electricity, so we also lost the Internet. And so we sat in the dark in the shelter and listened to the explosions, not knowing what was happening outside at all. Good thing was that I had a PowerBank, only it was only two-thirds charged, and it would have been enough for five charges on my phone. But we had nine adults with phones. It's good that grandmothers are not very active smartphone users, and did not ask for a charge. But Yulia and Lena and I really wanted to be in touch and see what was outside, at least when the alarm ended, and we could go out onto the porch, raise our hand up and catch some kind of signal.

Without electricity, I became quite sad. Dark and boring. There were worries about whether we could run the boiler without electricity. I had a good heating boiler, not modern, but good, it was ignited by a spark plug, but I did not know whether the spark plug was electric or not. Kostya knew this, but Kostya was not around, and there was no connection to call either.

The children also began to act up, because it was also boring for them to sit in the dark, when it was still early to sleep, and there was nothing to do. Lena began to read a book to them under a flashlight, but not everyone wanted to listen to her. It was so much worse when the lights went out.

In fact, we were so used to electric and that it's always there at the touch of a finger. And on the rare occasion it did fail we could always call for a repair man. Julia tried to find information on the Internet, where to call about the fact that there was no electricity, found several phones, tried to call, but there was no answer. I began to think what to do if the light did not turn on. It was necessary to save the battery of the phone, and I switched it to economy mode and just put it in my pocket. I had several flashlights with which we went to the forest, but they did not have batteries.

Last summer, the batteries were thrown out, and the flashlights were put in a box to wait for the next summer. The summer was still far away and new batteries had not yet been bought. I wonder if there are still batteries in stores, why I didn't think to buy them in advance, because it was already known that in some areas there was no electricity. Why do I still think this can't happen to me? I hit my forehead three times in frustration. In the sideboard there were two candles that were used during our wedding ceremony with Kostya. The priest said to light them when it was very tight in family matters. And Kostya, however, sometimes lit this candle for several minutes during a big quarrel. Perhaps now is the time to light one of them, I thought, I took it and carried it to the kitchen. That evening we cooked dinner under our wedding candles.

Maybe that's why that evening God had mercy, and when the children were sleeping, the electricity was turned on. Electricians were working somewhere on the street. They drove under alarm and repaired power lines. I believe that these are also heroes who most likely will not be talked about in the news, and who will not be given a medal for courage. And I would give a medal for courage to those electricians who, in these difficult days, went to calls and repaired wires. And if an electrician is reading this book now, then thank you very much for your work and bow to the ground.

We immediately put on charge all the gadgets that we could. I put PowerBank and my phone on charge and decided that from this day on I won't stop charging PowerBank at all so that it is always 100% charged. I fell asleep thinking about tomorrow's trip to the pharmacies and the search for batteries...

10. The cat ran away

At night two grandmothers had a fever, I had to give them Nimesil, a powder that relieved fever and treated inflammation. It was a very good medicine, I kept it in the house for such emergencies. But I only had three portions, and I used two of them. The third one was kept for myself. You can blame me, you can blame me, but I understood that I could no longer get such powders, and if my temperature rises, then there will simply be nothing to bring it down urgently. I didn't say I had another one.

When we got up in the morning, I again gave my grandmothers paracetamol, made hot tea and they gargled their throats. But in general, of course, they did not feel well, and this bothered me very much.

When the morning shelling ended, we prepared breakfast and had breakfast. Grandmothers went to lie in their infirmary with a hot teapot. And I put on a down jacket, a hat, boots and a backpack, took a bicycle and went to the pharmacy.

Yes, the pharmacy in the center, which I thought was open, was open, but there were 30 people in line for it. Well, if they are standing, then there is something, I thought, and got in line too. There was a guy ahead of me in line who worked at the senior center. He asked the saleswoman for adult diapers of any size, but she only had small ones, and he said: let's at least fix these somehow. I also took disposable diapers. It was evident that he was very tired, but there was no anger and irritation in his words, there was only doom and determination that something had to be done and to use what was available. As I understood, there were about 20 old people in the center for the elderly. All the staff left, and there were two or three people who tried to take care of the old people, simply because they could not leave them to die. After an hour in the cold, I finally got to the coveted window through which medicines were given out, but it turned out that there were no antipyretic or anti-inflammatory drugs at all. There were no heart drops and pressure pills that grandmothers asked for either. I managed to take a few jars of sedatives on herbs. Thank God for that, because everyone in my house was really on edge, and I needed something to calm my nervous system. In fact, I dripped sedative drops to all adults in the morning and evening so that there would be no nervous breakdowns.

So, I was going to go home bringing nothing. But on the way I stopped at one of the supermarkets, there was almost no queue, and when I went into it, I understood why. Almost all the shelves were empty. There were only chips, crackers and Coca-Cola, not very popular in the besieged city. I looked in the place where the batteries used to be, but there were no batteries. I wanted to buy matches, but there were no matches either. In general, I left the store without purchases.

My cat Shadow and Fluffy the cat went to the toilet outside. Although they had a toilet in the house just in case, they did not really like to use it. When we were bombed again, during lunch, Shadow was on the street. They bombed somewhere very close and he must have been scared because he ran away. Of course, I hoped that now everything would calm down and he would return, because Fluffy ran home as soon as everything calmed down. I wonder where she hid herself during the bombing? Tom, my dog, also did not go to the toilet in the yard, he was waiting for a walk. But the other two dogs, Archie and Caesar, did not wait for a walk. And my yard very quickly turned into a public toilet. Of course, all this was unpleasant for me, because, despite the war, I liked to go out to drink coffee in the yard and look at the trees, how the buds swell. I decided to just bury what the dogs had done, but there was still frost and earth and what the dogs had done was frozen. I did not succeed, I had to wait for the heat. It's disgusting, but there's nothing you can do about it. Maybe it's unpleasant for someone to read about it and you say: why describe it at all? But I want to tell everything in detail, so that it is clear that the siege is not only a lack of food and constant bombing, but also a bunch of unpleasant little things that you can't get away from. This is all additional little stress that accumulates and depresses a person. And with constant stress, such little things can lead to a nervous breakdown.

On this day, the city center was heavily bombed. And when during the next bombing we were sitting underground, I received a message from a friend that my store was blown up. All this, of course, is material and acquisitive, but I created my store when I was on maternity leave with my eldest son, and it grew and developed along with my eldest son, and I treated it like one of my children. I felt very bad, as if the life had really been taken from someone very dear to me. I wanted to cry, I could not find a place for myself, although there was no turning around in the shelter anyway. I went to the children, trying to watch cartoons and be distracted, then to Yulia to talk, then to Lena to look at some news, but it was all wrong. When the shelling ended and we left the bomb shelter, I went to the grandmothers' room and told my mom what they had told me.

– What can you do? God gave, God took. Do not be upset, it's good that it was the store, not the house. – Mom said. But I couldn't calm down.

– I'll go and see while there's no shooting, – I said.

– Oh, look carefully, we are being bombed very heavily today. – Mom got excited.

– I'll be right back. – I answered and began to get ready. I really got dressed very quickly, took out the bike and began to pedal with all my might, despite the fact that my legs hurt. When I arrived at the store, it turned out that it safe as houses. I drove up to the front door, examined all the windows and doors – everything was in order, everything was intact, the shutters were locked. My heart was pounding like crazy, because there was still an entrance from the yard. I again got on my bike and went around the house on the other side, all the time saying: "Lord have mercy. Lord have mercy. Lord have mercy". And when I drove around, it turned out that everything was in order there. Then I got angry at this friend. Why write this? Well, okay, I would understand if they had hit this house or the house next to the store, but all the houses in the area were also intact!

They started bombing again. I got on the bike without stopping for a second and again began to pedal at full speed. On the way, I saw a line of about 20 people. It was so surprising, because the streets were completely empty, even the volunteer center under my store was closed. I moved closer and asked:

– Why are you queuing?

– They are selling cigarettes. – they answered. Yes, nicotine addiction is a serious thing. On the one hand, I understood these people, but on the other hand, I could not understand. After all, they bombed, they bombed very close. It was life-threatening, but they were in line for the poison, which also shortened their lives. Well, it's none of my business. The explosions were somewhere very close, so the ground shook under my bike. And it all seemed to me that I was about to fall off this bike. Sometimes I had to slow down the pace of speed in order not to fall, I had to keep calm. I drove up to the gate, jumped off the bike and began to get the keys out of my pocket, they, as luck would have it, clung to the lining. Then I inserted the key into the lock of the gate and began to turn it, but for some reason it did not go, probably my hands were trembling, but I exhaled, concentrated, pulled the handle and turned the key. I grabbed the bike, threw it inside, closed the gate and flew like a bullet into the basement.

– Well? – the girls asked.

– Well, the store is fine! – I exclaimed with annoyance. – I don't know what he was thinking about! Why write such things for nothing?

I was very angry.

Yura's neighbor's internet operator apparently repaired the breakdown on the line and we had internet again in the shelter. While we were sitting during this shelling, Kostya called on the Internet. I told him what I was told about the store and that it was false information. Kostya said:

– Don't be angry, people are all stressed now, he got confused hearing something somewhere, maybe he wanted the best, it happens, don't be angry with him, I'm sorry about the situation.

– What do you feel about the war from the very beginning? how do you live? – I asked – Tell me in detail.

– The first days of the war were not scary, there was a feeling that it was given by God that Tykhon and I were here, probably to pray for you.

God's concern is very acutely felt, there were thoughts that everyone might not have long left, and therefore it is necessary to forgive everyone and be as honest and clean as possible.

A very reverent feeling appeared to you, to tears, I wanted to pray for you, so that the Lord would strengthen you. I understand that it is very difficult for you and you have a big responsibility.

I feel joy for Tykhon, joy on the verge of the end of that life that left and will not return, a feeling of surprise and consolation that they met Ksyusha, a girl from Mariupol of his age.

Mostly we try to pray, but we also talk with the monks about God's providence. Monk Lazar said to allow Tykhon sweets (which made him misbehave, he was impudent, his mood changed, in the monastery it is felt better). Because it's not easy for him anyway, he worries about his relatives, and it's more difficult for him to console himself. Still he walked with Ksyusha, got acquainted with animals, learnt Psalm 90. And Monk Seraphim often told me that Tykhon should be instructed, that I should not to let him be capricious. There were many times that Tykhon helped me in obedience, and it was always gratifying for me and I felt happiness and peace that my son, our son, is able to be helpful and hardworking. The monks treated him with attention, Monk Zechariah showed how to bake bread in the oven when there was no light, it was a real adventure for Tykhon.

I feel awe in relation to the family and the importance of the fact that you are my family and peace and indifference about everyday things.

– Thanks for sharing your feelings. I really miss this, and for a moment it seemed as if you were near. And thanks for Tykhon, I'm glad that he has classes there so that he can be distracted.

– Friends have been calling. Their house was damaged, they asked if they could come to our shelter? They are very scared.

– Well, they can come. But they won't be able to spend the night in the shelter, there is no place there, there are children there. When there is shelling during the day, we hide there, of course. They will have to sleep either together on the same bed or separately on the floor. Tell them, if they decide that it suits them, they can come.

Later I found out that they loaded things into the car and went to us, but on the way they decided to try to get out of the city. Everything worked out well, they left the city.

Lena had two cousins in the territorial defense who knew where Lena and her children were, probably they called up and she told them how we live and with whom. I thought so, because in the evening the military called us and said that they had sweets and toys for children. The military who defended the city were receiving food, warm clothes and so on from all sides, people on the outskirts cooked hot food and brought it to the guys right to the position. And so people brought them sweets, they don't eat so much. I decided to share them with the children. I think one of Lena's brothers said that there are seven children in the basement, so they decided to bring joy to the children. The soldiers called Lena, she went to the bridge, took the packages and returned. We don't even know who they are or what their names are. The bags contained cookies, sweets and a few toys. We gave some of the biscuits and sweets to the children right away. They were very happy, laughed, put these sweets into their mouths. There were several toys, and Yulia said:

– Hide it, Nykon wi be hapoy to get it for his birthday.

Indeed, I thought. After all, the child's birthday is coming soon, and now I can't buy anything. We were going to invite his classmates and friends. The T-shirt which I ordered was not ready. But you need to somehow celebrate, give him at least some joy. And I hid these toys in the closet in my room.

The grandmothers continued to gargle and drink hot tea, but their condition worsened. I asked Yulia about medicines and she also found only a couple of powders, but this was also a help. To be honest, at that moment I was a little confused. What to do? What if it's COVID? What if they get pneumonia? They will die here in my house. I didn't know what to do, nothing came to mind. The only thing I could treat them with was salt and jogging. But grandmothers are not children, you can't make them run around and clear their throats. And their body is different, jogging can only make things worse. With such heavy thoughts I went to bed.

When my mother was young, her favorite movie was "Gone with the Wind". And in this film, the main character Scarlett O'Hara had a very wonderful phrase: "I will not think about it today, I will think about it tomorrow." My mother used this phrase regularly and taught me to do the same. So, I took off my socks, crawled under the covers, closed my eyes and said:

– I'll think about it tomorrow...

11. I change shoes for medicines.

Instead of good morning, explosions of Russian artillery burst into my ears. I jumped out of bed, threw back the covers, opened my eyes and started uploading reality into my brain. Reality did not want to be loaded into the head, the brain desperately resisted, claiming that this was a dream. Not a dream, I convinced my head, pulled on my socks, put the phone in my pants pocket and left the room. Grandmothers in the hall also opened their eyes.

– Well, how do you feel? – I asked.

– She coughed all night. Didn't you hear? – My mother said.

– No. Slept like the dead. I'll make you tea, I'll bring it now.

All the children, Yulia and Yura and Lena and Vitya slept in the basement as always. They closed the entrance only with the grate so that heat and air would come out of the kitchen. A friendly sniffing was heard, probably, explosions were not heard underground. I made tea for my grandmothers and coffee for myself and sat down to think. The fact that I was able to find food almost every day is good, but the amount of money in my pocket was slowly melting away. And in order to get medicine for grandmothers, I think even more money will be needed. Money can do anything, and I decided to take care of that first. I had a whole shoe store. I donated part of the winter shoes to the territorial defense and volunteers, but it started to warm up and maybe someone needed sneakers. I posted on Facebook that I can drive up and open a warehouse if someone needs shoes. And do not judge strictly, I will make a discount but I will not give it away for free, because I have 16 souls in the basement and eight animals.

After breakfast, I decided to go to distant pharmacies that were not on the main streets, but on more distant ones, perhaps there was still something left. Since now we had flour and I got up anyway, I baked pancakes for everybody. 3 liters of dough for pancakes was made by me. I had breakfast, put crackers in my pocket, a backpack on my shoulders, got on my bike and went to more remote areas. There was usually little bombing between nine and eleven in the morning, and I was going to use the entire period of time.

While riding, I noticed a garbage truck. It struck me. They worked, despite the bombing and sirens, they took out garbage from the city. Heroes who will never be given a medal. Thanks to them, the city was not drowned in garbage during these difficult days. I noticed that the garbage containers were right on the road at its edge so that the garbage truck could pick them up quickly, without stopping in the courtyards of the houses.

I wandered around the area, looking for pharmacies. I went to one pharmacy – it was closed, to the second pharmacy – it was closed, to the third pharmacy – it was closed, to the fourth pharmacy – it was closed. This is where I started to get frustrated. And when I was already desperate to find a working pharmacy, I began to pray to God: "Please, Lord, I really need medicine". Suddenly the phone rang, a friend, Sergey, called.

– Maria, I saw your Facebook post, I need sneakers, because mine are completely falling apart from constant running around in melting snow. How are you in general?

– Oh, Sergey! I've been looking for medicine all morning, my grandmothers got sick, I don't know what to do.

– Listen, we have a large working pharmacy here in the area, I'll run into it, if I buy something, I'll meet you at your store in half an hour, okay?

– Well, of course.

It's not an easy task to ride a bike from one part of the city to the center to the store in half an hour, but I pressed the pedals and rolled. In general, for all these days on a bicycle, my legs had already begun to gradually get used to this mode, they no longer hurt so much. When I arrived at the store, it turned out that Sergey was already there.

– Here you are. I took everything I could.

And he handed me the package. I looked inside and was stunned: there were three packs of cold powders with paracetamol, two for adults and one for children.

– Thanks, Sergey! You have no idea how important this is to me right now.

– We have to stick together. It's the most important thing now. Let's pick up sneakers, as I also have to go home to my wife and children.

– You are not going to leave?

– Where should I go? And how? There is no green corridor, and there never will be. I'm not ready to run into Russians somewhere and lose my wife and children.

We quickly picked up his shoes, he immediately put them on and ran. In the following days, two more people applied with a request to open the warehouse, so we improved our finances a little.

While there was no shelling, I decided to go to the old district and look for my cat. It took the sane amount of time to go home and to the old district from my store. Cat Shadow often ran there for a walk on peaceful days, and there was a high probability that this time he ran there too. I came to the old district, began to ride around the houses and call Shadow. Met my former neighbor, asked about the cat. He said that he did not see Shadow for a few days. I also made a circle around the high-rise buildings and rode back. "What if he is no longer alive and I don't even know about it?" – I thought, but immediately drove away these thoughts. This is my Shadow, he will not disappear.

And so I went home without the cat, but with a full backpack of medicines. The mood was wonderful, there was silence in the city, the spring sun was peeping through the clouds. But when I came home, I saw that in front of the house water was pouring from the sewer pit. I flew into the yard, into the house, into the toilet – yes, someone had not checked the barrel. The water that poured God knows how long in a continuous stream completely filled the pit. I shouted something at the children in annoyance, because I thought that most likely it was them. I went into the room, sat down at the table and almost burst into tears. Now it was impossible to go to the toilet in the house. It was impossible to wash dishes in the sink, let alone wash or do laundry. I sat in complete detachment trying to come up with a solution to the problem, but apart from the sewer nothing else came to mind. We had a spare pit in the yard and in peacetime there were thoughts of making a switch to this pit, but there was already a confirmed project for the city sewerage and this spring we were supposed to be connected. I told Kostya that it makes no sense to engage in this nonsense, as long as we just call the sewer more often. I started looking on the Internet for the phone numbers of all the vacuum trucks that came to hand, and wrote to all of them, but there was no answer. I wrote about 10 phones on a piece of paper and planned to try to call them every hour, maybe someone will respond.

– Don't be so upset. Let's go to the street. – Mom tried to calm me down.

– I don't want to go outside, it is -5 there! – I couldn't calm down. – By the way, I got you some medicine.

I took the bag of medicines and gave each grandmother a powder and told them to drink. Aunt Tanya tried to refuse, for the reason that I might need it more. I looked at her as sternly as I could and said that the ground was frozen and there was nowhere to bury her. I was joking, of course, and she realized that I was joking, took the powder and went to drink. I told them to drink four of them a day. She said that they still have enough.

Lena came in to find out what happened to the pit. I angrily told her what happened, for some reason I suspected it was her children. I guess I wanted to find someone to blame then. Lena, thank God, had enough willpower and common sense not to be rude to me in response, but to take the initiative into her own hands:

– What can be done?

– Here are the phones, call them, maybe someone will answer.

Julia ran into the room:

– Airplane! I saw the plane get shot down! Right in front of me!

– Where? – we ran out into the street. There were clouds of smoke in the sky.

– I was just standing on the street. Suddenly a plane flew by, and I saw one rocket, it flew by, and then another one and an explosion and the plane began to roll somehow and flew over the horizon. I never thought that I would be able to see something like this.

– Well, get ready, now they will take revenge. – I said. – Let's quickly eat and get settled in the shelter.

We didn't wash the dishes, we need more time to wash it in the wash basin, we decided to leave it for now. Vitya tidied up the cobwebs in the street toilet so that the children would not be afraid to go there, but they were still afraid. And it was necessary to go before the shelling, there was a hitch, the children were capricious. Nykon was used to this, he sometimes ran there when he walked in the yard, but Lenin's children saw such a terrible toilet for the first time. Little Katya even refused to go there, but it's easier with her, they put her on a pot in the house and then poured the content out. But Rada had to be persuaded.

Grandmothers ate, drank medicine and lay down in the hall to watch TV. They did not go down, so as not to infect the children. You cannot imagine how scary it is when the earth and windows tremble during the bombing, it seems that now everything will collapse, but the grandmothers were ready to endure it. The health of children was more important than their own safety.

A group appeared in Telegram and Viber, which reported when the air raid began or ended throughout the Chernihiv region. Since the power lines were damaged and the siren in the city no longer sounded, people in the city learned about the air raid alert from these sources. When it was reported that an air raid had begun, we all went down to the basement. We sat and talked. Lena called and wrote to all the sewers, of which only three people answered. They all said that the drain in the city was closed, so they are not working now. When I began to ask to come at least to pump out and pump into another pit, no one agreed anyway. You can understand them, why risk your life because of other people's slops?

While we were looking for the phone of the vacuum trucks, I looked on the Internet, there were a lot of messages from volunteers that they were raising money for helmets and body armor for the military. This situation still persists. You come to the recruiting office, they take you to the army, they give you a uniform and a machine gun, and that's it. To protect their lives, soldiers buy equipment themselves or their relatives buy it. Now this has already been established, there are special sites, there are people who bring bulletproof vests and paints for sale, but at that time it was hard to get all this even with money. I looked at these ads, and I was hurt and offended. After all, these soldiers are someone's husbands and fathers, but I could not help. I had a small amount of money, but I also had 16 people to feed. Now I regularly give money to volunteers that I know personally, because now I am safe and I know what I can count on, but then I did not know what would happen next.

Nastya called, our good friend, who also had three children, and said that she now has buckwheat in the store here, if we need it, she can take a few kilograms, although the price is twice as expensive.

– Of course, take 2 kg. Why are you in the store? It's an air raid! – I almost screamed.

– They give buckwheat! Understand? Buckwheat!

– Yes. I understand.

When I hung up, I picked up a prayer book and said:

– Let's pray that nothing happens to Nastya and other people in the store.

Everyone nodded in agreement, and I read a prayer.

When the shelling ended, we went outside just to get some air. The children again wanted to use the toilet and began to act up again, especially the girls. Lena persuaded Rada that there was no other place, but she almost cried at the thought of going to the cold old barn and taking off her pants there. Then Victor turned to me:

– So what, nothing can be done with the pit?

– I have a cesspool like Septic, the water eventually goes into the ground, you just need to occasionally throw bacteria so that they eat everything. I think that in a day or two the water will go away a little, and it will be possible to go to the toilet at least for the children and for us at night. I have another hole in the yard, but we never made a switch to it.

- Show me. – Vitya said.

I led him to the hole in the street, we moved the lid, the hole was full to the top. Of course, all sorts of sewage floated there. Then we went into the yard, moved the stove, there was an old pit, it was almost empty.

– Maybe I can bail out one hole and pour it into another?" – Victor asked.

– How will you do it? – I raised my eyes to him.

– Using buckets.

– So you will scoop with a bucket until the night.

– Let it be till night. My daughter is crying, she doesn't want to go to the terrible toilet. – Vitya said confidently. – Give me buckets that you don't mind giving for that business and off I go.

Since there were no other ideas at all, I gave him two old buckets, and Vitya cheerfully set to work. He picks up two buckets in one pit and carries them into a pit in the yard, about 25 m, pours them out, and goes again. Picks up, goes and pours out. I stood next to him and joked with him. I don't know what else to talk about in such a situation, well, we just joked about everything, on this topic. He walked with buckets for more than an hour. Vitya was physically strong, but still, it must have been very difficult. Plus, he got all dirty while carrying, slop spilled on his pants and sneakers, but he still walked and carried buckets from pit to pit. It is also worth remembering that it was the beginning of March outside, and the temperature during the day was positive, but not more than five degrees. I don't know how he didn't get sick after that. It seemed to me that the water practically did not decrease. The pit was really wide, but after an hour of work, I saw the result. Of course, it was no longer possible to fully use the sewer, but at least children and adults could go to the home toilet at night. I washed Vitya's pants and sneakers right from the hose on the street, because it was impossible to enter the house in this. I found Kostya's jeans and Kostya's sneakers for him so that he could change into dry and clean clothes, and we washed his jeans and sneakers in the wash basin.

From that day on, we also washed dishes in the wash basin and poured water into the garden. No one even thought about taking a shower. But we still had cold and hot tap water, and that was good too, in many areas of the city it was no longer there. We still had electricity and the heating was on regularly. We didn't even starve, food, of course, was not the same as in peacetime, but we didn't go hungry. In general, it was possible to live. And it was frightening. You can even live like this...

12. Our area is being bombed.

New day, new worries, new hopes. The grandmothers got better. Of course, they still continued to drink medicines, but it was clear that they were getting better. This made things easier, at least, there was no need for urgent actions and decisions. I got on my bike in the morning and went to Nastya's for buckwheat. For some reason, in emergency situations, our people first of all buy buckwheat. And now it disappeared from the store shelves on the very first day, and the fact that Nastya managed to get it was certainly a miracle. Thank you very much for not forgetting about us, Nastya, you were probably so surprised that there was buckwheat that you immediately thought of your closest friends. Healthy porridge is easy to prepare, you can eat it with milk and sugar as breakfast cereals, or as a side dish with meat or vegetable gravy. We met with Nastya on the way to each other, she gave me buckwheat, and I gave her money.

– Well, how are you?

– We are sitting. Most of the time in the basement. When they don't bomb, I take the children outside for a walk, because you can go crazy with them.

– Are you going to leave?

– Not yet. Gasoline is now very hard to come by. Vasya and I deliver bread around the district. We go to the Grain Plant and deliver to people in need.

"Amazing!" – I thought, another experience of how people found a way to be useful in a difficult situation. We stood for a while and then went home. Subsequently, when it became very difficult, Vasya took Nastya with three children to the west and now she is also in Europe. Probably, then it seemed to all of us that it couldn't get any worse, and since we can live in such a situation, then we will survive, but every day it got worse.

I returned home, everyone was already awake there. The morning was suspiciously quiet and the children did not hesitate to run around the house. Lena was on the phone again. And Lena is a vocal and guitar teacher by profession, and in general they have a very musical family. And my son Nykon went to a music school and learned to play the guitar. So I decided to offer Lena an activity to distract herself:

– Listen, Nykon's teacher gave notes there, just before the attack, and they still haven't sorted out a new melody for this reason, maybe you can figure it out with him?

– Let's take a look, it's also interesting.

We lowered the instrument and the sheet music down to do this while we were forced to sit in the bomb shelter. Now the children were so busy, during the lull, that we did not want to distract them. But we already knew that this lull would not last long. A person gets used to everything, and we established a life with breaks for sitting in a bomb shelter.

– Air raid! – Yulia exclaimed, running into the kitchen – the children quickly went to the basement.

She regularly checked the Viber group that wrote about the air raid, she now had such a function to monitor the beginning and end of the alarm, because the sirens were no longer working. We went down to the basement and began to just talk with Yulia, and Lena began to learn a new melody on the guitar with Nykon. There was something in it. After all, usually everyone is running somewhere, in a hurry, doing something and just giving time to children, there is always not enough time.

I sat talking with Yulia, and scratched my head, I had not washed it for probably a week, and before that I just rinsed in a basin.

– I itch all over. Maybe I already have fleas?

– Don't talk nonsense. – Julia said. – You just need to wash. My pit is not full, let me turn on the boiler for you, go take a shower with hot water when there is a period of calm.

– Great idea! How did I not think of this before?

– Yes, I somehow didn't think about it myself being busy with all this thing going around. And in a good way it would be necessary to bathe everyone in turn, one person per one calm period, so that in a few days we will all bathe.

When the air raid alert was cancelled, I climbed over the fence to my neighbor and went to the shower. It was very cold in the room. They now lived with me and almost did not heat the house. I immediately prepared a towel and clothes so that I could immediately dry myself and get dressed. I locked the shower and turned on the hot water. What a blessing it is when hot water runs through the body! I melted like that for about five minutes, just enjoying it, unable to stop. But the distant explosion of a shell that reached me brought me back to reality. I quickly soaped, rinsed, dried myself, dressed, pulled on a hat and jacket and climbed over the fence to my house. But this feeling of purity! I was just happy at that moment.

I got a call from my sister in America. We were not blood relatives, but our mothers were friends and we grew up together and for me Alena was a sister.

– How are you?

– Sitting in the basement, scared.

– It's kind of a nightmare. How is this possible at present?

– The world has gone mad. Forgot. For a long time there was no big war, and we forgot. Having forgotten about God we live well and without problems, and we breed some kind of quarrels. Now everyone will remember what is really important. How is your mom? – I asked. The fact is that in 2014 I took my mother from Donetsk, and Alena could not pick up her mother and younger brother, there was something with their documents.

– They are bombed every day too. They still have total mobilization, they catch people right on the street and recruite to the army. My brother just turned 18, his mother hides him in the basement.

– It's a nightmare, of course. At least they don't catch us on the street, they only spread summonses. Many go to the army on their own following their hearts, some just leave the place.

– I want to help you with money. I believe you can still buy something in some shops. Send me your bank details.

– Good. – I decided not to refuse and not to resist. If my sister wants to help, then we should give her this opportunity. I sent her bank details. She really suffered there with the transfer, called back several times and clarified, but everything worked out. I thank her very much. I'll have to go shopping tomorrow and spend the money if I can find anything. Maybe even equip grandmothers next time, let them take a walk in the fresh air and also bring something. Grandmothers, by the way, were getting better, they still sometimes sniffed, but no one's temperature rose.

– Grandmothers! I think you need to shower. While there is no shelling, quickly go one by one to Yulia to have a shower. After the illness, after the temperature it will be very good.

Grandmothers tried to resist, aunt Tanya said that she still did not have clean clothes. But I insisted, gave everyone clothes from my stocks. My mother and mother Galya were about the same size as me, but grandmother Tanya was taller. It's good that oversize things came into fashion, I just bought myself a sweater a few sizes larger – it fit Tanya's grandmother perfectly. The pants were a bit short, but they fit well at the waist. Grandmothers took turns getting clean clothes, a towel, shampoo and climbed over the fence to the neighbor's flat and then back and dried their hair with a hairdryer. It turned into a conveyor of grandmothers, and then grandfather joined. Within an hour, the entire elderly population of our shelter was clean and dry.

While the grandmothers were washing, it was just quiet, but I knew that this would not be for long. In fact, I was very tired mentally and physically. I went to the computer to check the mail and decided to turn on the music for a while. But when I quietly turned it on, such a cheerful dance one, I wanted to dance so much that I turned it on full blast and began to dance. Lena came, looked at it for two seconds, and then, silently, without saying a word, she also began to dance. Then, children got out of the basement and ran up and began to dance too, jump around and squeak. I turned on the New Year's garland, which we still had not removed, because the children liked to turn it on in the evening. And we got a whole disco. We danced, forgetting about everything, it was very cool, it relieved stress very well. But another air raid drove us back underground along with a good mood.

Lena's brother called from the territorial defense and said that he would come in an hour.

– May he? - Lena asked.

- Yes, certainly. It's even very good. – I answered. But when her brother arrived and went into the yard, it turned out that he was with a machine gun. For him it was natural, but for me it was somehow scary and wild. He was going to come into the house, but I didn't let him in. I don't know if I did the right thing or not, but I really didn't want a man with a machine gun to come into my house. It doesn't matter whether it was our man or not. Maybe I did wrong, then forgive me. But I had to make a decision, and I made a decision that there would be no man with a gun in my house. I thought that he would just leave the gun on the street and go in himself, but he said that they should not leave weapons unattended. Then Lena simply took the children out into the yard, and they stood and talked there. Her brother talked about the need to leave, that a breakthrough of the ring was expected and that it would be necessary to leave at that time so that she was ready. But Lena did not want to go, she was very afraid. How can you be ready to take three children and a dog under your arm and go somewhere? At that moment the brain refused to accept it.

When I sat down to have dinner, Fluffy, Nykon's cat, was lying on the next chair. I wanted to throw her off, but she only meowed in response and lay back down. It seemed suspicious to me, I took her in my arms, and she squealed very plaintively. I put her on the floor, and she was somehow very crooked and limping with difficulty. It was clear that something was wrong with her. Maybe she got poisoned, or maybe one of the children crushed her, maybe even broke her paw. But there was no veterinarian, there was no one to ask. I picked her up and carried her to my room. My room was the only one where the children did not go, because I forbade it, there was my territory, a place where I could rest so as not to go crazy. Dymka, my mother's cat, I removed from the room not to interfere with Fluffy. I gave her food, but she didn't want to eat. I tried to give her water, but she also refused to drink. Oh no! As long as I'm here no one dies! I went to the kitchen, took 10 ml of milk into the syringe, took the cat by the withers and poured it into her by force. I still don't know what's happening to her, but I know for sure that she needs strength.

I was sitting on the bed petting Fluffy when a huge explosion rocked the house. I jumped out of bed, couldn't figure out what to do for a few seconds, then ran to the kitchen. Everybody had already fled and descended there. in my house. I ran to the grandmothers.

– Quickly down and without talking! – I almost screamed.

It became clear that our area was being bombed. Another close explosion, from which the house staggered and the windows rang, left the grandmothers no choice. Tom jumped desperately near the hatch, and I desperately called him. Then I could not stand it, jumped out, grabbed him in my arms and wanted to go down with him, but he broke free and ran a couple of steps, began to bark, but did not want to go down. Another close explosure made me understand that I didn't have time to persuade the dog. We all went downstairs, and I closed the hatch to the shelter, not as usual with a wooden grate, but with a wide wooden board.

It was very scary. It was just really scary. Very, very, very scary. Everyone was seized with animal horror. Lena began to lament. Someone else began to fuss. The ground was trembling so that it was impossible to stand on it. In order to somehow calm everyone down, I took a prayer book and began to read, first the 90th psalm, and then the 23rd, and the 26th. Many, and even children, knelt down and began to pray, plaster fell from the ceiling, and my voice trembled, but I continued to read one psalm after another to distract myself and distract the others. This nightmare lasted about an hour, but it seemed to me that a week had passed, these minutes dragged on so terribly and painfully. I read a prayer, and I myself looked at the second exit from the shelter, which was packed with rags so that the heat would not come out. I kept wondering if we could all get through it if the house was about to collapse. I also thought whether someone had blocked this exit from the outside with something heavy so that the heat would not come out. There were a lot of thoughts, from the simplest to the most terrible. But at one point it all ended, the earth stopped trembling and silence fell, only my voice continued to read the prayer. This time I was not in such a hurry to go upstairs, I kept listening to see if the explosions would start again. But, after some time, we decided to get out and see what was there. Tom the dog happily wagged his tail when we emerged from the hatch and I was also very glad that nothing happened to him.It was already dark outside when we got out. We went outside and saw across the road that several nine-story houses were on fire.

– Oh my God! There are people there! We urgently need to go there to help! – I began to speak, seriously intending to run there and help people.

– Stop. – Yura said sternly. – It's a curfew on the street, we can't go out anywhere. You can be shot at the nearest checkpoint without asking why or where you are going. There are special services in the city that deal with this, – Yura said firmly and confidently.

He was right. But it was so terrible, watching the houses burn down and not being able to do anything. I stood and watched, and could not tear myself away, tried to listen, maybe someone was calling for help. But I calmed down only when I heard the sound of a fire engine approaching. Now I could calm down, I believed that they are professionals and would do everything that was needed.

I went to my room. I felt very bad. Maybe I got sick, or maybe it was after a shock, but for some reason I was in a fever, there was such a condition as if I had a temperature: weakness, chills, a headache. I decided to take paracetamol powder, just in case. I didn't even measure the temperature, I just diluted it with water, drank it and lay down on the bed. There, in the same position, Fluffy lay. I wondered if she also heard the explosions, maybe she was so bad that she could not go anywhere, or maybe she was not afraid. I cracked off a quarter of a paracetamol tablet and made her eat it. Then I brought another syringe of milk and poured it into her again. She tried to get up and jumped off the bed, but meowed loudly as she did so. It was clear that she was in pain, and it was clear that she needed to go to the toilet. I picked her up and carried her to the bathroom. Poor thing, she was barely able to do her business. After that, I wiped her paws with a damp cloth and carried her to my bed. Today she will sleep next to me, so that if she becomes ill, I can help her with something. I felt so sorry for her. I just lay and stroked her and slowly fell asleep.

13. Nykon's birthday.

It was quiet in the morning, but I still woke up around 6 am. I didn't feel well, I felt weak, dizzy, my whole body ached. "I mustn't get sick," I thought, and went to the kitchen, prepared some cold powder and returned to the bedroom. Fluffy was still lying next to me on the bed. In the middle of the night, I once again carried her to the toilet when I woke up from the fact that she meowed and tried to climb over me. I stroked her and she blinked back, as if to say yes, thanks for your concern, but I'm too sick to be silent for too long. I broke off a piece of Paracetamol again and gave it to her. Then forced her to drink a little milk, by force holding her by the withers. And she lay down again with a displeased look that I disturbed her. Dog Tom spent the night in my room and tried to lie between me and Fluffy, he was probably jealous that I paid more attention to the cat than to him. I stroked him a little, but asked him to lie down at my feet.

I had a few money orders left in the mail, for sneakers, and it would be nice to pick them up somehow, it is not known how long all this will last and how much money I will need. I began to correspond with the support service, they said that none of their branches is working in our city yet, and it is not known when it will work, but I can send documents via Telegram and transfer money. I spent about half an hour doing this, hoping to get money, but in fact I received the money about two months later.

I went to the kitchen, my mother was already there.

– Congratulations on the start of Lent!

We are Orthodox Christians and once a year during Lent we pray and do not eat meat for forty days.

– Likewise. Will you fast?

– It depends, – my mother answered, – in such a situation, as in an illness, it is allowed not to fast.

– I think we will eat what God will send. What are your plans?

– I wanted to go home to get a gift for Nykon.

– Did you prepare a present for him?

– No, of course not. But I'm thinking of giving him a music box, which he likes very much.

– I support the idea. Let's go while everyone is still sleeping.

We got up and went to my mother's apartment. It was early in the morning, and surprisingly, it was quiet.

We had little cash left by that time. It was on my bank card, and there was money that Alyona sent, but they didn't sell anything in the store which we could buy using a card. There was a message on the Internet that in the morning from 10 to 12 at the Ukr post office one could get a pension, but I could imagine what kind of queues there would be. I think the queue should be taken from early in the morning in order to have time to receive your pension before 12. I looked at all the ATMs on the way to my mom, but they were all turned off. So it will be necessary to make a bicycle raid around the neighborhood to find a working one.

When we were passing the first school by, we saw people with suitcases and children. I went to find out why they were standing there, and people said that in the morning there was an evacuation bus and they said that there could be more buses so they were sitting and waiting. I noted for myself that there was an evacuation point near the first school, but I needed to find out more precisely what and when, somehow I didn't feel like sitting in the cold for several hours with a child.

When we had already reached my mother's entrance, and she went into the house, I decided to go to the central market, in case the ATM was still working there. And surprisingly, it really worked. I withdrew the money that Alyona had sent, as anyway it did not give out more than that. There was a limit for withdrawing money per day. I returned to my mother, she had already found the box and tried to clean something up. It was quiet and surprisingly sunny on a spring day. I wanted cleanliness and order so much that my mother and I decided to tidy up. We began to collect the fragments in flour bags and take them outside to the trash cans, there was already a lot of garbage and broken frames and burnt furniture – people were putting their apartments in order. So we cleaned the kitchen and the room, but the balcony remained. But we were so carried away that we decided to clean it up, but we didn't have time to clean it up, because they began to bomb the city. Remembering all the horror of the last night, we quickly grabbed the box and ran home. But they bombed another area and we ran home relatively safe.

When we got home, Nykon had already woken up, and we arrived just in time to congratulate him and give him the box. While he was brushing his teeth, I slowly took out the hidden toys from the wardrobe and handed them out to the other children so that they could congratulate Nykon. The toys were simple and not quite for his age, but he was still happy. Children came up and congratulated Nykon, hugged, wished whatever they could think of. And then he, along with the rest of the children, climbed into the basement and began to play with these simple toys as if they had not seen toys for 100 years. And about half an hour later, just between two periods of shelling, there was a knock on the window, I looked out and it turned out that Oksana and Kostya had brought a cake to Nykon.

– We couldn't leave a child without a cake on his birthday! – Oksana exclaimed.

– But how did you find the products?

– I did my best to prepare this surprise! – Oksana answered with a smile. They had been searching for necessary products for several days, specially for Nykon's cake. – Well, show me the birthday boy.

We went into the house and called Nykon. Of course, he was delighted, a real cake, and even with the inscription "Nykon is nine years old" – just a fairy tale. Another shelling began, and we lowered the cake underground.

– Can you stay with us until the shelling is over? – I asked Kostya and Oksana.

 – No. We have already got used to it. It's even calmer when it's not in a stone bag, – Kostya smiled.

They got on their bikes and rode, and I went down to the basement to cut the cake and congratulate the birthday boy. We have never celebrated a birthday in such a close circle.

A friend who was in the territorial defense wrote, asked to see if his apartment was intact. He lived just across the road, near the school that was bombed last night. I promised to go see. When the shelling ended, I got ready, taking advantage of the break, to go see my friend's apartment. Misha came up to me:

– Can I go with you? I'm so tired of this basement!

I looked him up and down and agreed. Since I was going to go there, it means that I think it is safe there. We left the house, crossed the bridge and first of all went to my friend's house. It was in this house that a rocket hit yesterday, and we saw this house being on fire. Only it got into the apartments on the upper floors, under the roof and into another entrance. Roma's apartment was on the second floor, and nothing happened to it, even the windows were not damaged.

When we entered the courtyards of the nineteenth school, there was, of course, a lot of destruction. We got to the nineteenth school, where the pool and the dining room were destroyed. There were holes in the residential areas, and there were nine-story buildings here, I saw a man in the apartment on the second floor, who was throwing the remains of furniture from his apartment from the balcony. People were walking everywhere, there were men from the territorial defense who kept order. The fragments hit the cars that were standing near the houses, there were many small holes in them. Not far from school 19 there was an Internet provider building with many antennas. I don't know for sure, but maybe they were aiming there? They didn't hit, they only destroyed the parking lot with their repair machines, and a pile of twisted metal remained from the machines. Misha looked at everything with wide eyes. He took out his phone and put it away.

– Would you like to take a picture? – I asked. – Do it. Now it's not an emergency, you can do it.

We did not walk for long, I was afraid that shelling would begin, and Misha would be very scared, after all, he was still a child. But everything was quiet.

When we got home, there was a fuss. Lena's brother called and told her and the children to get ready, that they would come, pick them up and take them out of the city.

– What should I do? To go or not to go? – Lena almost screamed.

– Of course you should go! It is not known what will happen next. Remember last night. And the end is not yet in sight. Save the children.

– We will go by Gosha's car, only his windshield flew out from the explosion. He'll be here in half an hour, can you tell me the exact address?

– Sure I can. How about Vitya?

– I won't send them alone. - Victor said firmly. – I'll go with them, at least to the border. If they don't let me out, at least I'll be sure they're safe.

The commotion was terrible. Lena tried to find and collect all her things, her husband and three children. I helped her get ready. Rada, the eldest daughter, had bad shoes, and I gave her Tykhon's UGG.

– If your boots fall apart in the middle of the road, then you will remain barefoot in winter, – I persuaded Rada. She did not want to go in someone else's shoes, and Tykhon's UGG were too big, but after our arguments, she agreed. We had a few dry rations, we kept them in case of emergency, but I decided that now is just such an occasion. What to give them for their trip so that there is food, and it does not deteriorate? Of course, dry rations and cookies!

We loaded Lena with a whole bag of food, because it was not known how and how long they would go. Lena decided to leave some of the things at my house, they didn't take too much with them. Another shelling drove us into the basement. We sat and discussed the upcoming trip. Lena, of course, had many fears, but I tried to calm her down, because her brother is with the military, and they know where there are exits from the city. Then I already began to understand that I needed to get out of the city. Lena tried to persuade me to go with her, but I refused. Where will I go when there are so many people in my house?

When the shelling ended, Gosha drove up to the house in a car. The car did not have a front windshield, and Gosha was dressed very warmly and even (I don't remember well) had some ski goggles. We quickly loaded things, children. Then they tried to wrap up the children, because they had to take them into the cold in an open car. They also took the dog Archie with them. Finally everything was ready, Lena hugged me and burst into tears. Again she tried to persuade me to go with her, but I told her to pull herself together and get into the car, especially since Gosha was starting to get nervous.

They left. I felt empty. Immediately it became so quiet and empty in the house.

Everyone was somehow discouraged, and I was also depressed... Different thoughts were born in my head: "Maybe I need to leave… Why am I sitting here? It's already clear that nothing will end in two days. Well, how can I leave wjhen I have people in here? What will happen to them without me?"

Tykhon's call freed me from these sad thoughts.

–Hi, mom, I miss you so much. I was going to visit you today, I packed my backpack. – very excited, almost crying, Tikhon chattered, – I'll come to you on foot, I've already decided.

– My dear little son, be patient. There is no passage to the city. Are you really that bad?

– No. It's very good here. I got a girlfriend here, she teaches me to read a prayer, the 90th psalm, I almost completely learned it. One monk yesterday taught me how to bake bread. Can you imagine? Real bread in the oven! They also showed me how cottage cheese is made from milk, it hangs in gauze for a long, long time until all the water drains. We rode a horse-drawn cart into the forest. There are so many interesting things, come to us, I will show you everything.

– I can't, son. They surrounded us on all sides. It is impossible to enter and leave the city, so we will sit here for the time being.

– Dad says that his friend went into the city, that there are roads, so we can go.

– It's too dangerous, Tykhon. Be patient, please, I love you very much, just be patient. We will definitely catch up.

My heart just broke. I really wanted to cry, but I was afraid to show my feelings in front of my son, so as not to alarm him even more.

My heart was very anxious, the sun was setting. A car drove up to the gate, Yura came up and took some box and returned to the house. After some time, my mother Galya came up to me and whispered in a conspiratorial whisper:

– Maria, Yura brought some electronics, it's dangerous, now the Russians will understand that we have electronics and a rocket will be launched at us here. Tell him to take it away.

– Mom, don't worry, it's unlikely that Yura would bring into the house something that would threaten his children. But I'll figure it out.

I went up to Yura and asked what kind of device it was. He replied that the guys from work asked him to set up something related to the Internet.

– This is not dangerous? – I asked, I myself did not know what they were afraid of. Yesterday they bombed the ISP building across the road, suddenly they somehow figure out where the signal is coming from us?

– Well, at least don't get hysterical, there will be no signal, I'll just set it up, and the guys will come and pick it up. – Yura answered firmly.

– Okay. You know better if it's dangerous or not. – I went to do things which had to be done.

Mom Galya several times approached me with a frightened look and wondered if it was safe, the general tension affected, the nervous system simply could not stand it, and she was looking for a reason to worry.

Already before going to bed, I decided to call Lena, to find out if they even got to the outskirts of the city. But when I called her, it turned out that they were at home. Today they just managed to go to the gas station, there were very big problems with gasoline, and Lena's brother, through his connections, took them to refuel the car with gasoline. They decided to spend the night in their house in the basement of Vitya's workshop and try to escape from the city early in the morning. "Well, then everything will be all right today, there is nothing to worry about", – I decided and went to bed. But when I came in, I saw Fluffy, she was lying curled up, I completely forgot about her having too many worries. So I returned to the kitchen, took a syringe with milk and forcibly poured it into her. She weakly resisted, it even seemed that she drank the milk with pleasure. Then I went and got another syringe and poured it into her again. Then I took her to the toilet, she obediently did her business and I took her back. I put her to my left, where Kostya usually slept, lay down next to her and stroked her. Falling asleep, I kept thinking about Tykhon: what if he really was going to walk from the monastery? He is so determined and courageous!

14. Lena left.

Thank you for the quiet morning on International Women's Day. Today, March 8, is International Women's Day, and it is celebrated in Russia, Belarus and Ukraine. It was quiet this morning, thanks for that. I was able to not jump out of bed, and even stretch. In peacetime, I would wake up with hot coffee and flowers that my husband would bring. And then the children would run into the room and bring their drawings or some small handmade gifts. Today, I can just pull myself up in bed, such a gift.

Fluffy blinked and stretched beside me, looking like she's getting better. I began to stroke her, and she moved closer to me and murmured very loudly with pleasure. Her rumbling is very annoying at night, but now it was like stress relief. We lay together with her and relaxed, because today is our day.

I remembered that Shadow, the cat, was missing next to me. Usually he was there when I woke up, I stroked him and then we went to the kitchen together. I took the phone and wrote a Facebook post about the lost cat, if anyone sees, let them call. Hope, of course, was not enough, who now cares about cats when people die. But it was necessary to do at least something: what if someone saw him, or maybe saw him dead, at least I would know his fate.

I went into the kitchen, where, as always, grandmothers were in charge. They came up with something for breakfast, drank tea, discussed the coming day.

– We need to withdraw money from an ATM, – Galya's mother said, – do you know where the working one is?

– I know. I can go and withdraw if there is still money there. You collect the cards for me and wrap each card in a piece of paper, and on the piece of paper write the code and the amount to be withdrawn, I'll go as soon as I have coffee.

– Understood. – Grandmothers said and went from room to room. While I was drinking coffee, each brought a card with a piece of paper and a code on the piece of paper.

I also went into the room, gave Fluffy milk to drink, and then gave the tail from the fish and she ate it. But after that she lay down again, it was clear that she still had little strength, but now I knew that everything would be fine. She jumped off the bed, was about to go to the toilet, but I decided to carry her to save her strength.

I got ready, got on my bike and rode towards my parents' house. I didn't try to drive through the main street anymore, there was a checkpoint there and the guys didn't really like it when people drove past them. I drove across the avenue where the grocery stores were. One of them was open, I decided to go in since I was in the area, especially since there was no queue. I went to the store, but it was empty, all the shelves were empty, only there were several packs of chips and ketchup near the checkout. I looked at the empty shelves, did not understand anything, unfastened my bike and drove on. By the way, I always fastened my bike, because the means of transportation now was worth its weight in gold and it would be very unpleasant to be left without a bike at such a time.

When I drove to the intersection of the main streets and drove towards my parent's house, I began to meet men with flowers who were coming from the central market. It was so wonderful and so strange. I just smiled at them and they smiled back, I don't know what they were thinking. But I thought that even at such a time, someone went out to sell flowers, and someone got out of the basement and went to buy them. Life goes on.

I drove up to the ATM, it worked, I looked around, because it was in the corner, and not on the main street, and I was afraid of bad people who could see that I was withdrawing money and take it away. I very quickly inserted one card, dialed the code, withdrew money and put it in my pocket, inserted another card, dialed the code, withdrew money and put in my pocket and the third and fourth in the same way. I don't know how I managed to remain calm, but I remember for sure that it was very scary that now someone would come up from behind. But everything worked out, I got on the bike and went home. Already on the way home, I noticed that the cars were parked on the road towards Kyiv, but it was about 2 km from the parental apartment before leaving the city. That is, there was a two-kilometer queue to leave the city. I hope Lena had already left, they were still going to leave since yesterday evening, they had everything ready. I decided to call her, but she didn't answer right away.

– Where are you? – I asked without further ado.

– We are in line at the exit of the city.

– But it's almost 11:00, why didn't you leave earlier?

– Well, first my brother's wife was late, then there were some other problems, as a result, now we are standing in a line.

– I see a bunch of cars, everyone is waiting. God help you! If you do not have time to leave, come to spend the night. – I said and hung up, there was nothing more to talk about. So, deciding to leave is one thing, try to get out of the city first and what's next is generally unknown. But I began to have thoughts that I need to do something. And think about getting out too.

When I got home, everyone was already awake. The grandmothers had already gave the children breakfast. Nykon ran out to me with a drawing:

– Congratulations, mom! He screamed and hugged me.

Surely it was the grandmothers who reminded him that today is Mother's day. But for the kids, it was a chance to have some change. Misha also drew a picture for his mother, I took a picture of it and sent it. Then called his mom and let them talk. Misha went to another room, but I could hear him sobbing, he also missed his mother very much and cried.

I gave money to my grandmothers. They thanked being very excited. I think it was very important for them to know that in case of emergency they have money. Grandmother Galya and aunt Tanya approached me with a request to take money from them for food.

– I have enough for now, thank you, – I answered, it seemed inconvenient to me to take money from grandmothers at such a time. Okay, if I really didn't have any, yes, but so far I had money, and Alena helped, and there wasn't much to spend it on. But the grandmothers insisted, and they had such longing in their eyes that I suddenly realized what I needed to take. That they will then feel better. It is important for them to make some contribution to the common cause. I took half of their money, I said that was enough.

After lunch, I decided to take a walk with Tom towards the center. It was such a wonderful, spring day and the whole day was relatively quiet, only on the outskirts of the city some explosions were heard far, far away. Good thing that I kept him on a leash. The silence was broken by the whistle of a mine, and they began to fall, it seemed, somewhere not far away, because it was very loud. Tom got agitated and began to tear from the leash, I could barely keep him by my side. I sat down, and squeezed his body between my legs, and covered his head with my hands and head. So we sat with him for about 10 minutes under a tree in the hope that the mines would not fall on our heads. In general, there were a lot of reports that dogs ran away, they were very afraid of explosions. Later I found out that during the shelling the heads of dogs are tied with a scarf so that they are not afraid, but at that moment I didn't even have a scarf with me. When the shelling ended, we jogged home.

At home, everyone was already crawling out of the basement after the shelling.

– Where were you? Why don't you stay at home! – Mom attacked me.

– Well, it was quiet. I decided to take a walk with Tom.

– You'll find your trouble!

It was obvious that my mother was really scared. The explosions were very audible, so they were somewhere very close.

I remembered Lena and decided to call her, dialed once, twice, but there was no answer, and I wrote her a message on Viber in the hope that she would read it when there was time. And, of course, I began to worry, it is not known what could happen under fire on the road. There had already been a lot of cases described on the Internet when columns leaving the city were simply shot or blown up. Moreover, there was no agreement on a green corridor from Chernihiv, and the military said that most likely there would not be. That is, people today traveled at their own peril and risk. Of course, there was information from the military that there was a way to get through. But this way for travel, firstly, could be closed at any moment if the Russians go on the offensive, and secondly, many roads are shot through by the Russians from both sides. So I was very worried about Lena.

A friend called, from a city in the north, their city was captured by the Russians. She said that they have tanks freely moving along the street, Russian soldiers go into houses, where they want to stop and spend the night, take what they like. Not all of course, and not everywhere, but there were cases, and this keeps the whole city in suspense. Their communication towers were also suppressed, the only operator through which it was possible to communicate was MTS, because this company had branches in Russia and Ukraine, as I understood it. Nobody brought food to the shops, and the shops were all closed, it's good that the city mostly consists of private houses and everyone has cellars with food supplies. The Russians hacked into several stores and took out vodka. Local residents tried to arrange a rally in support of Ukraine, but they were dispersed by automatic bursts over their heads. Some were arrested and taken away in an unknown direction. This ended the resistance. It became clear to everyone that there would be no democracy there.

At that moment Fluffy came into the kitchen and sniffed the bowls.

– Oh, alive. – I said.

One of the children immediately wanted to pick it up, but I did not allow it.

– Wait, let me come to my senses, though please, be careful she is still small.

Fluffy was only eight months old, just this spring in April I was just going to sterilize her. And now she was almost a kitten, given her small size, and the children loved her very much, but it was scary that they would start squeezing her again. Mom's cat Dymka and Aunt Tanya's Milka kept away from children's hands, they were wayward and did not let strangers take them, especially children. But Fluffy was an affectionate and purring little cat, and that was dangerous. I took her in my arms and put her in a place behind the boiler, where the heating pipe went, Shadow and Fluffy liked to sit there very much, and the children would not reach them.

Shots were heard outside the window. There was such a roar, it seemed that they were shooting on a neighboring street. By this time, I already understood when they were shooting at us and when they were shooting from us. And I also understood that if they shoot from us in the next street, then in half an hour our area will have no stone left unturned. I put on my shoes and ran out into the street, it seemed to me that they were shooting literally from around the corner, I ran there, but there was nothing there, I looked into another street, but there was no one on it either, maybe they shot and left? Why exactly am I running? Well, let's say you saw that on the next street there is a launcher that shoots at the Russians, what will you do? Are you going to scream out? How will they generally regard your shouting? Maybe you are for the Russians, and you prevent them from shooting, or maybe you are crazy. I don't know, but it was very scary. I wanted to do something. Our military defended the city, I understood everything, but I really wanted to protect my house.

And so, not finding anyone, I returned home and began to prepare for the bombardment. If they fired from us somewhere close, then they will also shoot at us somewhere close. I immediately turned on the heating boiler at home, because it is not known how many hours we will have to sit in the basement, it may take all night. We quickly cooked some kind of porridge, handed it out to the children and climbed into the basement. The dogs stayed in the kitchen. I thought it was safer.

They bombed somewhere very close, the whole house was trembling, and again we all sat and prayed. Now our destinies were only in the hands of God.

By nine o'clock everything was quiet in the street, we went out into the yard to listen, somewhere in the distance we could hear automatic bursts. Although it was heard very well in the night air and silence, we already understood that it was somewhere on the outskirts of the city. But after such artillery preparation, we feared that they would decide to go on an assault at night. That evening it was very hard for me to fall asleep, machine-gun bursts were constantly heard outside, and sometimes shots and explosions. It seemed to me that now the Russians would storm, and it would be necessary to run to hide in a shelter. What if they come here to the house? Even the dog Tom, who was lying under the window, flinched from the explosions, grumbled and rolled over. This made me even more scared, because I believe that animals feel danger better than we do. But fatigue still won and I fell asleep.

15. There is no more electricity.

In the morning, too, they bombed heavily. Tom even climbed onto my bed and I didn't chase him away, I understood that he was scared and I was scared too, but I didn't want to climb into the cellar. Tired, I'm already tired. During the morning bombing, power lines were damaged, and our electricity was completely lost. I charged the phone from PowerBank and put it in economy mode.

After breakfast, my sister from Russia called.

– Well, how are you?

– All the same. Only the bombings are intensifying, automatic bursts are heard. Here the electricity is gone. The stores ran out of food, I don't know what to do next. But I have a reserve of five days, and then we'll think of something. How are you, what do they say?

– They do not talk about Chernihiv in the news at all. They talk about Mariupol, they talk about Kyiv, they mention Kharkiv, but nothing about Chernihiv, as if there were no fights there.

– Well, there may be no fighting in Chernihiv, but lately they have been bombing from morning till evening. What do people say?

– People get angry. Their sons and brothers are dying there, and they are angry at the Ukrainians for killing their children. All these sanctions only lead to the fact that people will become even more angry at the whole world in Russia. The unity of the nation is certainly good, but I would like it to havw other slogans. Our guys are dying, young guys, my city has already had ten funerals, of course they are buried with honors as heroes, but this doesn't make it easier for mothers.

 – Can't mothers keep their sons out?

– You do not understand. There is such propaganda. Here Russia is almost the savior of the whole world from Nazism. And young boys easily believe such an interesting idea. It hurts and embarrassing.

– Yes. It hurts and embarrassing. Young boys are dying from both sides, it is not clear for whose interests.

– Everything is being cut off here, including our networks and communication with you. What social networks are you on? To keep in touch.

– There is Viber, and in Telegram I will write to you not to get lost.

– I don't know what else to tell you.

– You don't have to say anything. Let's just pray for this to end soon. So that, despite someone's interests, people simply stop dying. This is so scary...

I remembered that there really were fewer and fewer products left and I had to look for something. I decided to go to the nearest stores and see if my store is still there. I found the groceries in a stall in the middle of the block. Small entrepreneurs got food somewhere, through their own channels. The prices, of course, were higher, but I personally did not blame them for this. It is clear that now, in order to bring them, it was necessary to go by car, and not wait for delivery. And for your car, you still need to get gasoline, and the price for it was also higher. I managed to take fruits: apples and bananas, so the children will be happy. And cheese, there was expensive cheese, which in normal times is not so often bought, but now money is starting to cost less and less, and cheese is a very high-calorie product.

After I bought groceries, I decided to take them up to my store. And when I rode up, I was stopped by one guy who was collecting humanitarian aid.

– Oh, hello, Maria, is your store open?

– Well, it depends, if someone calls, I'll open it. Do you need shoes?

– Yes. It's getting warmer, and I only have winter boots, and with all this running around, they begin to deteriorate. Can you open the shop now?

– Of course. Just go to the back entrance so as not to disturb people.

I opened the store, I didn't have to turn the alarm off, there was no electricity in the store. That is, if someone would decide to get there, then it would be possible to endure everything calmly and without nerves. I turned on the flashlight on my phone, and under the flashlight I picked up the young man's running shoes. He was not too picky and wore the second pair I suggested.

– How much? – he asked.

– Do you have money? – I was surprised.

– Of course. I'm not some kind of marauder. I understand that everyone needs something to eat.

– So that's great.

I made a small discount and took the money. Of course, they were not superfluous to me.

I closed the store, got on my bike and rode back home. The streets were completely empty, it felt like the city had died out. When I rode up to the river near the house, explosions began to be heard, which meant that it was necessary to enter the house faster. Lately, they had been bombing very close to us, and it was not known at what moment the shells could arrive in our area. But it looked like it was about to happen. There was a feeling that, well, this time it would definitely hit us. Therefore, I left the bike literally right behind the gate and, without undressing, went down to the basement, closing the lid behind me.

– Something happened? – Julia asked me.

– They're bombing. – I answered.

– You just rushed in like they were bombing our street.

– I have a feeling that they are bombing our street. Although, perhaps, it only seems so. Nothing new, usual thing. – I explained as I took off my jacket.

It was still warm in the basement, although with no electricity none of the heaters were working now, and it was only a matter of time before it got cold here. People were sitting with flashlight. Misha played on the phone, Nikon watched him play. I kept hoping that the repairmen would fix the line and the electricity would appear. When the explosions ended, we went out into the yard to listen if they were shooting. And what we heard scared us very much. On the next street there were sounds of passing tanks, the creak of trucks on the asphalt.

– What is it? – I asked Yura in a half-whisper.

– Tanks. – he replied whispering too.

– Ours?

– I do not know. Should be ours. Too early after the shelling for them.

Well, since our tanks are moving through the city along the next street, then perhaps they are trying to cover them. So we stood and reasoned with Yura in half-whisper until the sounds of the tracks died away in the distance. We are not military men, we do not understand either tactics or strategy. Given that there is no electricity and practically no communication, we were cut off from the world and did not know for sure what was happening outside. Sometimes there were some messages on the Internet, from which we understood that Chernihiv was still holding out, but naturally the military did not report on the Internet how it was holding on and with what forces or in what directions. And we did not know on what day and at what time it might turn out that Russian tanks would enter the city.

We returned to the house and went about our normal business. My grandmothers and I began to cook dinner, counting right away that we would cook tomorrow and the day after tomorrow, if today we use this and that. Since the electricity was never turned on, Yura brought a large battery from home. It weighed 15-20 kilograms. It was very large, heavy and old, but it was filled with electricity, Yura took care of this in advance. Everyone stuck their phones in with great joy. Especially Misha, who was completely bored in the basement without a phone. Previously, at least they had a laptop working there with movies and cartoons. Yes, and we, too, without a phone actually had nothing to do and be distracted. What is the use of sitting without light, without occupation?

I decided to find a use for myself. I had a friend who worked in a hospital before the war and I called her

– Hello, Natasha, listen, do you need help in the hospital?

– No, thanks. We are coping. We are doing well so far. Try calling the central hospital, maybe they need someone, but I think there are enough hands now.

Given the communication problems, we did not talk for a long time, found out what was needed and hung up. Later, after I left, I contacted her and found out that when everyone started to leave, most of the hospital staff also left. Natasha and a few other employees stayed for the whole department with bedridden people. They looked after them, washed them, cooked food for them on the street on fire, and all this under constant shelling. I asked her then why she was not evacuated, and she got angry. Well, yes, who needs half-lying corpses from the cancer ward, when women and children are beaten indiscriminately. If I had then found a use for myself, then most likely I would still be in Chernihiv.

There was no news from Lena, and after lunch I decided to go beyond the bridge and try to contact her. Tom was sitting by the door, as always. It feels like he was following me, whether I go or not, whether I call him with me or not. I looked into those faithful, puppy eyes and said: "With me." And he jumped, began to wave his tail in full readiness to go with me, even to the edge of the world, no matter what. When I crossed the bridge and entered the courtyards across the road, I was struck by a large number of fragments. There were no traces of explosions, perhaps they were in other yards. A lot of windows flew out from the air waves after the explosion, and maybe even from a flying plane. I remembered how my parents' house shook when the plane flew over it. I began to call Lena, first just on a cell phone, and then via the Internet. I don't remember how many times, but she finally answered.

– How are you?

– We are on the train, going to Lviv. Everyone is alive. It was, of course, very hard to come by. Yesterday it took all day just to get to Kyiv. We were driving through some fields, Gosha was constantly urged on, and his car was old, and even without a windshield, it was barely moving. He explained that if he tried to go faster, the car would simply stop, and we told him to go faster otherwise we would remove his car from the road ourselves. It was very scary, mines were heard somewhere, I had never prayed like that before. Everyone was afraid that Gosha's car would stop, and we would stay in an open field to spend the night with the children in a car without windows. By nightfall we reached the outskirts of Kyiv, gasoline was running out, we decided to stop by for a gas station. It was already dark, probably the curfew was beginning, there was a checkpoint, and the soldiers said: "Stop, otherwise we will shoot!" and I shouted: "Don't shoot, there are children here!" I put my hands up and walked towards them. They let me in, figured it out and we drove to the gas station. It was already dark, and the night shift tanker left us to spend the night in the shop hall, between the rows of chocolates. We put a blanket out of the car and spent the night like that. And in the morning, my brother's wife said that the easiest way is to go to the railway station, and trains go west from there. Gosha did not want to leave the car and drove, probably in the direction of Vinnitsa, and we arrived at the railway hall. It's just a crazy house here, 1000 people who are trying to leave with children, with animals, bags, such an overcrowded place. But we finally found out where the train was and got inside. We rode on top of each other, packed in like sardines.

– Thank God. Alive. Healthy. So everything will be fine.

– What do you have?

– Bombed from morning to evening. Today the sounds of tanks could be heard in the next street. I don't know what will happen next. Scary.

– I told you, come with me.

– Well, how can I go? I have people.

– And what, it would be better if you were all hooked there together?

– I do not know. I'm thinking it over. Okay, go with God. Write sometimes how you are and where.

While talking with Lena, lost sight of Tom.

– Tom! Tom! – I screamed.

But he didn't run out. I nearly paniced. I can't lose my dog! Where will I look for him?

– Tom! Tommy!

I ran through the yards again and again shouting his name. Tears began to choke me, it seemed that I was about to burst into tears. But around the next turn appeared Tom. As if nothing had happened, he sniffed the bushes. At my appearance, he raised his muzzle, looked and again began to sniff. I got angry and yelled at him. I don't think he understood anything from my cries, he only understood that I was angry and lowered his tail. I put him on the leash and we went home.

The electricity was never turned on. We ate under the lanterns. The question arose of how to light the boiler. I began to try to light it with a torch, but I did not succeed. When I called Yura to show it, he simply pressed the piezo and the boiler caught fire. It turns out that the ignition button did not depend on electricity.

– Hooray! – I said, and added fire. But in order for the water from the boiler to pass through all the pipes in the house, we had a small pump that pushed this water through the pipe. Here it is, just powered by electricity. Two pipes went out of the boiler, one of which was with a pump, and the second with a valve. Previous owners said that water can flow through pipes without a pump, but simply because of the temperature difference. That is, if the pump did not work, and sufficiently hot water accumulated in the boiler, then the valve opened, and the water flowed through the pipes under its own temperature difference. We hoped for this, but after 20 minutes it became clear that water without a pump does not want to go anywhere by itself. We tried to connect the pump with Yura's battery. The pump began to work, the water went, and we already wanted to calm down, but then the battery finally used up all the charge and turned off. The batteries in the rooms began to warm up a little, it was cool in the rooms. Yura began to try to deal with the boiler. I called Kostya, but Kostya confirmed that the valve should work. We have never checked the valve and the previous owners most likely did not use it either, because with the pump hot water passed through the pipes much faster and the house warmed up faster. Yura realized that it was just a valve, most likely due to the fact that it was not used, it either rusted inside or turned sour. He began to frantically pound on it with a hammer. I turned the gas on and off, tried to start the battery, it turned on for a minute, the pump worked and turned off again. I watched this for about half an hour, but there was nothing I could do to help. First of all, I'm not very good at all of this. I just sat and watched Yura spinning around the boiler, knocking, then turning it on, then turning it off. But, in the end, he succeeded. Part of the pipe behind the valve began to warm up, which means that the valve opened and water went through the pipes.

– And if the valve closes again by itself, the boiler will not explode? – I asked Yura.

– I'll sit by the boiler for a couple of hours until the house warms up, and then turn it off. Go, go to bed. – Yura said calmly and confidently. I knew he could be trusted with this. I turned around and went to bed, because it was already about ten and I was absolutely exhausted.

16. They take water from in the river.

I woke up with a jolt and jumped up on the bed. For a long time I could not understand what happened. And when I got it, I calmed down and got angry at the same time. It turned out that when I went to bed yesterday and closed the door, my mother's cat Dymka was in the room, most likely she was sitting in the closet. It could be seen in the morning that she decided to go to the toilet, and the door was closed in Tom's room. Tom is actually a peaceful dog, but probably wanted to check what was the matter, and Dymka began to hiss at him, hit him with her paw, and out of fright he jumped onto my bed.

– You'll drive me crazy! – I said reproachfully to Tom. And he stood on the bed, waving his tail and looking first at me, then at Dymka, as if asking what was going on in our room. I got out from under the covers and opened the door for the cat. The room was cold. I touched the batteries – ice cold. I got dressed and went to the kitchen. There was no electricity and the boiler did not work. I turned on the boiler, the water began to warm up, but the valve did not open in any way, I did not dare to knock on it when everyone was sleeping. Simply, I turned off the boiler just in case, and when I made hot coffee, I climbed back under the covers.

I looked at the phone, Ukrainian operators were not working. I caught some network from roaming. The network appeared, even the Internet appeared. I flipped through Facebook. There were very few posts from friends, probably due to the fact that there was a bad connection, and some did not have it at all. There were very disturbing reports from Mariupol that the city was blocked and there were problems with food. People were literally starving. I began to think what I would do if suddenly our food ran out and we were starving. Well, there were a lot of ducks in the river near my house, but they still needed to be caught. Tom came up to me, and he, by the way, wanted to eat. And I had a thought whether I could kill and eat my dog if me and my children were starving. They were so terrible, these thoughts, that to this day, when I remember it, I want to cry. But then I seriously thought about it. Thank God I didn't have to make those decisions.

When everyone woke up, we began to think what to do without electricity. It was necessary to charge the battery, and I knew that my parents had electricity in the house. There was no water, no heating, but there was light, and we decided to go there to charge Yura's big battery. The battery was very heavy and it would be crazy to carry it in your hands. At first, we tried to attach a bag with a battery to the bike, but it hit the wheels and there was a danger that it would be damaged. And then dad drew attention to the pram standing near our gate, which Lena left with us when she departed. Great, we decided, loaded the battery and went to our parents' house. We arrived, the battery was put on charge, and I also put my phone on charge. The temperature in the apartment was the same as outside, very cold. And for some reason my phone categorically did not want to be charged in such conditions. To charge it, I had to put it in my pocket and stand near the charger. A few hours later we loaded the battery back onto the pram and drove home.

When we left the entrance, we heard that in the next entrance, somewhere at the level of the third floor, a cat was screaming desperately. Perhaps the owners closed it and left. Maybe he was already dying of hunger and thirst. I thought about it, but did nothing. Now, when I remember it, I think that I had to look where it could be, try to drill a hole through the wall to let it out, but this is already now, when I am sitting in a warm room on the bed. And then I was just very sorry, but I went on my way. I saw on the Internet a video of a guy from Kyiv who went and rescued cats from houses, cutting a hole at the bottom of the door, I don't know if anyone in Chernigov did this. Surely, many animals died, just like that, locked in apartments. I know that there were people who rescued dogs left by the owners on the chain in private houses. The animals were very exhausted, and some did not expect being helped.

While we were in the area of my parents' home, there was a good connection, and Kostya got through to me. I picked up the phone. I started talking, and suddenly a woman ran up to me with a question:

– Do you have a connection? What operator works?

– Ukrainian operators do not work, roaming works. Go to the network, choose to select the operator manually, and select another operator that will be available, try this. Look for a place where there is a connection, sometimes it seems to be blown away by the wind. Today it works here, and tomorrow you can get it the street. – I told her.

And she went further, and the woman immediately took out her phone and probably tried to set something up.

– Well, what's new? - I asked Kostya going around the corner and stopping to talk.

– I'll tell you an interesting story. Zhenya called, the friend who brought me sunflower oil. He had a toothache, the flux blew out, and he is in Domnitsa monastery, as you remember. But he phoned the doctor, asked him for a visit and help, not for free, of course. Well, he went to the city on foot. And on the way, our lads caught him. They put a bag over his head, put him in a barn and beat him so that he would say that he was a Russian spy. And he, like most of our peers, studied in Soviet times in a Russian school. He knows Ukrainian, but speaks with an accent. And so he was tortured for twelve hours to prove that he was a Ukrainian. In the end, of course, they figured it out and let him go, but he had suffered enough fear for the rest of his life.

– Was his flux treated?

– Yes, I understand that it happened on the way back. Now he won't make a single step out of Domnitsa, he said so.

– That's a bright example for you, so that you don't try to come here. Okay, he was alone, and imagine going like that with a child?

– I tried to arrange to leave Tykhon in the monastery, under the supervision of Vladyka, and go myself.

– Kostya, don't be silly, please. You will go to no one knows where and you will disappear. Tykhon will stay there, no one will hold him back, he will also go somewhere. I beg you, be sensible, stay with our child in the monastery in safety. If something happens to you, I won't survive it.

Finally I came home. Yura looked at the battery, it turned out that we had only half charged it. Probably, it also did not want to get charged in the cold, like my phone. But it was enough to charge everyone's phones and there was still 15% left for the evening to start the boiler if the electricity was not turned on.

Not far from my house there was a small pine forest, it was called Yalovshchina. From us it was 1-2 km, not more. And today, all day long, the creaks of trucks were heard there, probably tanks, maybe other kind of artillery. Shots were heard from there, and then, probably, they got attacked back. What actually happened, I certainly do not know, I can only speculate.

After another shelling, when everything calmed down for a while, I decided to go to the old district and look for Shadow. I got on my bike and rode to my neighborhood, where I used to live, it was no more than 15 minutes by bike. When I crossed the bridge, I saw people who were taking water from the river. They lowered the bucket from the middle of the bridge into the river on a rope, because the water was cleaner there. Then they took out a bucket of water and poured it into plastic bottles to carry home. The water was brownish, but it was water. The high-rise buildings across the road no longer had not only light, but also water. People arranged toilets on the street, right in the yards.

I arrived at my old yard and began to drive around the houses and call Shadow, but no one came out. And then I met a neighbor from the house where we used to live, his name was Yura, I saw them the day before with his wife, she was pregnant. I told how we survive in my house and explained that Shadow had run away again, and I was going looking for him.

– Go to the basement, the entrance is on that side, people now live there permanently, maybe they have it.

Just at that time, shots began to be heard, and he went to the basement with me. I have never been in this basement when we lived in this house. When we entered, it turned out that about twenty people now live there permanently with their children. There was a central room in which there was a table and chairs, women sat there and peeled potatoes. I did not pay attention to what they cooked it on. Maybe they go home? But I went in, said hello, asked about Shadow.

– Yes. He lives here with us. He has a bowl in every room. Everyone feeds him. You call him, he's probably around here somewhere.

– Shadow, Shadow! – I said and went to the basement. There were mattresses and people lying in different rooms, someone was on the phone. But there was no Shadow. From somewhere out of the darkness two children came running, a boy and a girl. I knew the boy, Tykhon played with him in the yard, I said hello and asked about the cat. He said that he comes to spend the night with them, and goes for a walk during the day, they love him very much. And the girl said: "Please don't take him." I looked at her and realized that Shadow was needed here more. This child needs a bundle of warmth and affection, and I already have something to do.

– You wait, he will come. – One woman said.

– No. You need him more. I'll go home. Just write down the phone number, if anything happens, let me know at least.

We exchanged phone numbers and I left the basement. Shots were heard on the street from the side of the rampart. It was also possible to see the points of the rockets that go to the north – this was our artillery. So, the answer will come back soon, I thought, got on the bike, neighbor Yura stood still, waved his hand to say goodbye and also went home.

On the way back, I decided to visit a friend, Ira, who lived nearby. When I went to their floor, they had mattresses laid right in the vestibule, it was there that they spent the night with the whole family. Ira said that some people live in the basement of their house. But it's not a bomb shelter, it's just a basement, and she didn't see the point in hiding there. She said that she went down once, sat, but then she realized that it was too long to get three children ready and run down. They simply hid in the vestibule, between the apartments. She had three children: 17-year-old, 8-year-old and 2-year- old. Her husband traveled with volunteers and helped the elderly. We sat down to drink tea and I told her that I was thinking about moving out, because sitting in the basement without electricity and water is somehow very sad. Ira said that she was not going to leave, her house was here and she had nowhere to go and nothing to travel by, they didn't have a car. Just at that time, her brother arrived. He had a pizza delivery backpack on his shoulders, but when he opened it, we all gasped. There were four small dogs inside. The dogs were abandoned by the owners when they ran away from the city, and he took them and brought them home. Ira's daughter was delighted with the dogs, Ira was also not against replenishment. And of course, I thought to myself, this is just not enough. The thought to take one dog for myself stirred in my head, but I threw it away. If I have to leave or something happens to the house, then I don't know what to do with my own people, but here is a living creature, it's a pity, but who knows where to put it later. Of course, it was possible to take it, feed, and let God rule there, but I decided not to do this.

Ira left about a week after me, when a shell hit the house where they lived, just under her apartment, and all their windows flew out, the electricity, gas and heating were turned off. Naturally, they could no longer live there.

I returned home, there was Nastya's buckwheat for dinner, oh, and it seemed delicious. Yura again knocked on the boiler valve, trying to start it without electricity. The battery charge did not last long. And I took Tom, Nykon and Misha and Caesar and went for another walk, to the river. It's just when I arrived that Tom expressed his joy so much, he was so glad to see me, he rubbed against me so much, he looked into my eyes so much that I couldn't just walk away, he was like a younger child to me, and I had to pay attention to him. By evening, my legs were already giving up, but Tom ran so fervently and called me to go with him that I had to run along with him. Just near the river, I got a phone call. It was Yura, a neighbor from our old apartment:

– Maria, can we come to your house, me, my wife and a child?

– Child? – I did not understand.

– Yes, Masha gave birth to a boy two weeks ago, we had been waiting for him for 15 years and now we are sitting in a cold apartment without light and water.

– Lord have mercy! Of course come, collect things, go even now.

– Now we won't have time, the curfew begins, and tomorrow morning, as soon as the curfew ends at 6 in the morning, we will immediately go to you, can we?

– Of course you can, if you dial when you come up, I will help and guide you.

When I talked with Yura today, I didn't remember at all and didn't think about his wife Masha, that she was pregnant. If I remembered, then I probably would have called them myself, but it already happened the way it happened. We returned home, and I began to clean Nykon's room in order to put them with the baby there. The room is, of course, small and there is only one bed, but the second adult can be put on the mattress, on the floor. At least they will have their own space. Of course, this news excited everyone, because the child is two weeks old, and he is still very small. Everyone began to give advice telling to do this and that, and I said:

– Wait, let them get here. They will tell you what they need.

But when I went to bed, I also only thought that it was a little boy who was born two days before the start of the war. And when they bombed, I only thought that something bad would happen to their house tonight.

17. New settlers.

Explosions were heard all night, and in the morning I got on the Internet and saw that the Gagarin stadium had been bombed. The stadium where Tykhon played football from the first grade of school. Our Chernihiv team from the Premier League "Desna" played matches at this stadium. My eldest son ran with their emblem and the youngest too. It was somehow bitter and insulting so many moments were associated with this stadium in the five years that my children played there. When I was drinking coffee in the kitchen, for some reason the hamster squeaked, he jumped around the cage and climbed back into the house. We should feed him and attach the wheel in which he ran. We turned off the wheel at night, because when he ran in it there was such a crackling sound, similar to firing from a machine gun. Back on the first or second night, when they were still trying to lie upstairs, I somehow went into Nikon's room, and there Lena was sitting in an embrace with Vitya and frightened eyes. I ask:

-What happened?

- You hear, they shoot, they shoot very close.

I listened, but did not hear anything, and then I guessed that it was Shlepa, that was the name of the hamster Tykhon. We have already got used to the fact that he rumbles with a wheel, and did not pay attention.

 - This is Hamster.

- Which hamster? Don't you hear?

- Went. - I said and led her into Tykhon's room, where he frantically ran along the Slap's wheel.

- Your mother! - Lena swore - I'm already thinking that now the Russians are entering the city and they will shoot at us, and this is just a hamster.

Yes, fear has big eyes. - I said, calming down - go to bed, I will unhook the wheel.

And from that day on, I unhooked the wheel at night so as not to scare people. I threw some biscuit to Shloepa, checked the water and put the wheel back in place, and he didn't even eat, but immediately ran for a morning jog. They say that if they are not allowed to run, they will die, so let them run.

At the beginning of the seventh, Yura, a neighbor from the old apartment, called:

- Well, we're coming to you.

- Yes, of course, as soon as you get out, you will collect. - I said, and went to get dressed, so that if anything, I could immediately go out. Yura called back literally 10 minutes later, I was about to leave, but he said that there was an air raid and they were bombing in their area, so they would wait half an hour until the explosions were over, and then they would make their way to me. I offered to pick them up, but Yura said that they would come on their own, the main thing was to stop the bombing.

The electricity was never turned on. I got up to wash a cup of coffee, but the water barely ran, of course there was enough for coffee, but it looks like soon we will also draw water in the river. Coughs were heard from the basement, if only the children would not get sick again. Due to the lack of electricity, we no longer heated the basement. They only heated the house, and then only in the evening, when Yura could tap the soured valve with a hammer. It was spring, it was getting warmer, but it was still 7 degrees outside, and these 7 degrees climbed into the basement very quickly.

Finally Yura called:

- We are already near the church, come out and meet.

- I'm running! I said putting on my jacket. She said to Tom: "with me" and we went to meet friends. We met them right behind the bridge. Yura, his wife Masha and the long-awaited son. I'm ashamed to admit it, but I don't remember his name, forgive me friends. I took packages from Yura so that he could carry the stroller with the child across the bridge, because there were steps. And we quickly, quickly came home. At home, I showed them their room and told them to settle down. Then she conducted a briefing, showed where she was, talked about problems with the barrel and sewerage.

- If you need anything, just tell me.

Julia brought from her house a bath for the baby, she still had it from Dima. We had breakfast and were about to go to our parents to charge the battery when the city began to be bombed again. We all climbed into the shelter, I told Yura and Masha that there was an air raid, go into the basement and climbed, but for some reason they were gone for a very long time, they went down only after 10 minutes.

- Why are you taking so long? - I didn't understand.

- Well, while the child was dressed, while they dressed themselves, while they collected diapers and baby food, while they got water, so the time has passed.

 - Not. Will not work. - I said - So you will be late at the most crucial moment. Let's drop our jackets and extra blankets down here, and when there's an air raid alert, you just grab the baby in your arms and come down here, that's the right thing to do.

So we decided. When the bombing stopped, we were going to go to our parents to charge the battery. Yura from the old district said that he would come with us. We put the battery back on the stroller and drove off. When we were already approaching the intersection that led to the parental home, we saw a line of people near the store. We got closer, and it turned out that eggs were brought there. This is luck, I thought. We left Yura in line and said to take two trays of eggs, told where the parents' house was and went there.

And in the yard of the parents they put up a fence and dug out an outdoor toilet. Due to the fact that the windows were broken and it was still frosty at night, so that the pipes would not burst, all the water was drained from the system, that is, there was no water either in the batteries or in the tap. Accordingly, going to the toilet, and flushing was problematic. Carry a bucket of water to the third floor to go to the toilet, which still had to be carried to the house, of course, no one was doing this. Those people who remained to live in the house simply had nowhere to go, and they dug a hole in the middle of the yard between the trees, covered it with boards, and covered it around with some kind of burlap so that they could hide from people's eyes and go out of need.

We put the battery on charge and decided not to wait, but to come for it in the evening, so that it would not turn out like yesterday when it was only half charged. I also went to the ATM, withdrew cash, and went home. On the way I met Yura with eggs, he was a little upset. By the time it was his turn, there were few eggs left, and he was given only one tray (30 eggs).

 - Don't get upset. It's still wonderful. We didn't see them for two weeks. It will be possible to bake pancakes.

When we were sitting at dinner, Masha came out of the room, she was inseparably near the child, and now he fell asleep and she went out to eat.

How did it work out for you with your child? - I casually asked.

 - You know, we dreamed of a child for 15 years, everything did not work out. And then, finally, the Lord heard our prayers, and gave us a baby. I am no longer young, I barely reached the last month, I was in conservation. They put the date of birth on February 28, but he, Thank God, was born on the 22nd. It's good at least earlier, otherwise I would give birth in the basement, as girls now give birth. I saw recently in the news that they bombed and women in labor were also injured there. Just as the bombing began, we once went to the basement with Yura, but realized that by the time we got together, the bombing would already be over, so we were already sitting at home, not twitching and praying. It was only when the electricity, water and heating were turned off that it became very difficult. It's small at all, but I can't really wash it, I wipe everything with wet wipes. I still have it on artificial feeding, because as soon as the war began, my milk was gone, literally on the third day. It is very difficult to get food for babies now. Yura ran all over the city looking for it, and it is brewed with boiling water, and for me to make boiling water without light and gas, even though the howl of a wolf.

"Well, everything will be fine now. It's more or less quiet here, we still have water, gas. Yulia gave me a bath as soon as she sleeps, and we'll arrange a bath for the babies - children love to bathe. I remembered little Tykhon, how we, too, bathed him in a bath, with some useful herb.

After lunch, friends, volunteers stopped by, asked if they needed anything, I said that everything is there, if food for babies comes across, it would be nice. They said that there was a disaster with water, and almost no area is empty and people literally have nothing to drink. I still have water.

"So can we get you some?"

- Of course, but is there anything to gain?

- There are a couple of plastic bottles.

Let me see how much I have now.

And we got them a few plastic 6 liter bottles. They went to deliver to the yards so that people would have something to drink. Subsequently, they called in regularly, even when I had already left to get water. Our house is in a lowland and the water, although slowly, still flowed, probably flowed from the entire outskirts.

It turned out that the morning cough belonged to Misha. How did he manage to catch a cold again. I again made him water with salt and told him to get dressed, let's go, run with the dogs, cough, since you feel like coughing. We took two dogs, Misha, Nikon and dad joined us too. He was very fond of walking, as a child he walked 7 km to get to school every day and in any weather, so nothing could break him. We ran along the river, me, Misha, Nikon, and dad was a little behind because he was walking. The dogs ran contented and happy: first Caesar followed Tomik, then Tomik followed Caesar. And then, at some point, Caesar ran very far away. Misha began to worry and dad also walked faster, shouting his name:

- Caesar! Caesar, come to me! Caesar!

But the emperor did not appear. We began to worry and went in the direction where he ran away. And finally we saw him, Misha was delighted, but he cried out a little sobbing:

-Caesar! Caesar, run, come here.

And the emperor ran up to the pope with something in his teeth and laid it at his father's feet.

- What is it? I asked.

"A chicken," the pope replied, and Caesar stood contented and proud of his act and breathed wearily.

- What is Caesar, tired of porridge without meat? – Smiling, I asked.

- So what's now? Where to look for owners? We have caused damage to people. You have to pay.

- Dad, don't worry. In our area, chickens just don't run around like that, this is not a village, this is the center of the city. If someone keeps chickens, then they sit in the chicken coop. I think that when people left the house, they simply left the chicken coop open, because they understood that they would return and the chickens would simply die of hunger, and there is a chance that someone will survive on pasture. So we will not look for anyone, let them forgive. I raised my head to the sky and said: "You see, Lord, we are not from evil." Then she took a bag lying somewhere nearby, put the chicken in and walked briskly towards the house:

- Well done Caesar, we are with you for surelet's not get lost.

When we came home, mother Galya was, of course, also surprised, as well as the rest of the inhabitants of my house.

- Mom, the chicken needs to be plucked, gutted and boiled for the dogs.

- Let's do it now. Only domestic chicken, why only dogs?" she asked.

- Because the Caesar caught, but see for yourself.

I suspect that this particular chicken was in the porridge at dinner tonight, and not some other one that was bought in the store. But she is really domestic, she was simply killed not with an ax, but by Caesar. I was actually very happy. One could hope that with this hunter we would definitely not die of hunger.

After dinner, when Yura was again sorting out the boiler, and Yura and Masha were washing the baby, I went to my room and called Lena. She answered almost immediately. And I tried to call you all day, but for some reason the call did not go.

- Bad connection. It blows with the wind at times. I smiled. - Well, where did you get to?

We are in Poland, not far from Warsaw. Listen, there are such wonderful people here. We just arrived at the station, we were immediately met, everyone was fed, taken to wash, sleep, then fed again and taken to a certain house where we will live. And all with such care and love as if we were not strangers. There are a lot of Ukrainians in general, just thousands of people go and go. What about you?

- Bombing non-stop. There is no electricity, water barely flows. Stores and pharmacies are empty. We were also joined by a family of two with a two-week-old baby. Imagine, 15 years of waiting and waiting. Today we managed to take the eggs - a holiday. But it's getting worse and worse, and there's no end in sight.

"I told you, you should have come with us.

- Yes, where we would not fit with you, and even without the front glass. Maybe we'll get out somehow, I don't know what to do.

They started bombing again and the connection was interrupted. I went to the bomb shelter, Masha came out of the bath with a freshly bathed baby, I also climbed for the one wrapped in a towel. Her husband came down a minute later with a bottle of formula. Masha began to feed the baby. Now I regret that I didn't take a picture, such a picture: a woman with a baby in her arms feeds in the basement under a flashlight. And he ate and fell asleep, Thank God that he did not understand what was happening. It was getting cold in the basement, the heating from the house practically did not pass into the basement. Therefore, as soon as they stopped shooting, we carried the baby out of there. Misha sniffed, and I allowed him to spend the night upstairs with his grandparents, but in case of shelling I ordered him to immediately go to the basement. And Nikon was already sleeping curled up in a pile of pillows and blankets, I straightened him, laid my head on the pillow and covered him with a blanket, then thought and pulled a sleeping hat on him so that his head was warm.

Tom was very happy when I got out, he always met me from the basement with the same joy as when I came home from work. I scratched behind his ear, and he looked at me with his brown, devoted eyes. Today they had a royal dinner of porridge with chicken offal, everyone ate it with great pleasure. I launched Caesar from the street, he spent the night in his parents' room, it was very cold outside. And after that, we went to bed with Tomik. As always, he lay down under the window on the side where Kostya usually slept, he probably missed his owner. But I knew that at night he would crawl onto the bed on Kostya's side to sleep.

18. They bombed "Ukraine"

Boom! Boom! Boom!

I woke up from the explosions. It was dark outside. It was deep night. Bombs lay down somewhere very near. It was scary. I thought about going to the basement, but I didn't. I did not care. No, worse, I sat on the bed and waited for the bomb to fall and this whole nightmare to end in an instant. I was so tired, I was mentally and physically exhausted. I hoped the bomb would fall, I didn't want to live like that. "Blimey! This is what got me! I don't want to live! Have you lost your mind?" – I began a dialogue with myself. – Don't like life? Change! But I can't, it's not up to me. Do what depends on you! Think and do!" Explosions were heard again, I went to the toilet, drank some water and came back to the room. "You have to do something in order to live!" "I love life so much!" – I remembered my principle. Whenever I felt very bad, I remembered that I definitely love life very much, and if any thoughts that life is bad appear, then these are not my thoughts – they are from the evil. This is how I have been living for many years. "I'll think about it tomorrow", – I said to myself and went to bed.

Boom! Boom! Boom!

I woke up again from the explosions. Only outside the window it was already daylight, it was necessary to get up and live again. The shell never hit my house, which means I had to start a new day all over again: look for food, take care of loved ones, walk the dog. As I was already very tired, there was no longer the strength to endure, and the bombing intensified. There was no electricity for the third day, the water barely dripped. There were still some products, but it is not clear how long this will all last and whether I can still get any products.

I got out from under the covers, Tom also jumped up and joyfully galloped to the door. Probably, he, too, was scared and uncomfortable after the explosions. I went to the kitchen, my mother was already sitting there and drinking coffee.

– They are bombing all night, I can't sleep. – Mom said.

– Yes. I woke up too, put on headphones and fell asleep. – I answered.

– What are your plans for today?

– I'll go to your house now, I hope, there is electricity, I'll try to charge the phone and PowerBank. Maybe, I will withdraw more money, if I find a working ATM. What about your plans?

– Now I will cook something for breakfast, feed everyone, wash the dishes and watch a movie.

– Like in a sanatorium. – I joked. – Eat and rest.

I had something to eat and went to my parents' house. In order not to pass through the main street, where the checkpoint was, I decided to go around it through the library yard. But when I drove up there, a soldier was standing near the gate and said that it was strictly forbidden to go there. I sensed that something was going on, you never know what happened, and asked:

– What, people are not allowed going to the center at all?

– No, – the soldier answered, – you can't go through the library courtyard, go around the hotel "Ukraine".

– All right. – I said, but I thought to myself with annoyance: "You could have told me right away that I just need to go around!" I already thought all sorts of nasty things.

I went through another yard and went to Mir Avenue. The street was almost empty, there were maybe one or two people, although the weather was wonderful, quite spring. When I looked to the left, I saw bricks on Mir Avenue, at first I did not understand what had happened and drove a little closer to take a look. It turned out that they blew up the hotel "Ukraine". It was located in the very center of the city at the intersection of two main streets, Pobeda Avenue and Mir Avenue. I do not understand what made this hotel their target but half of it was gone. I stood there for a minute, looking at the ruined building, trying to memorize everything in detail. Probably, I will never forget this hotel or the fact that I just looked at the destruction. There was no feeling of pity or regret, just curiosity.

I arrived at my parents' house. It looked the same, although not quite as the windows of the entrance were clogged with plywood, most of the windows in the apartments, like ours, were clogged with cellophane. That is, people continued to look after their homes. I went upstairs, there was electricity in the apartment, and I immediately put the phone and the PowerBank on charge, wrapping them in pillows and towels so that they would not freeze. Then I went down to the street again, in my memory there were still memories of how the plane flew overhead, so I didn't want to linger on the fourth floor for a long time, I felt safer outside the building.

While there was time, I went to the ATM, which worked last time, but it was turned off. I drove even further to McDonald's, there was a central market and it turned out that people go there. The market, of course, did not work, but there were a lot of people in a hurry, from where and where they all went, I don't know. And there was a working ATM nearby, so I managed to cash out some more money. True, there was nothing in the stores, but if suddenly there is, then I will have something to buy, unless of course the hryvnia does not depreciate at all. I started thinking about changing hryvnias for dollars or euros, but where can you change it now?

I again drove to my parents' apartment, picked up the PowerBank with the phone and drove towards the house. I decided to go after all not by the hotel "Ukraine", but by the first school. And when I left the courtyards in front of the school, I saw a large number of people, around 40-50 people, who were sitting, standing, someone even lay down. I drove closer and asked the people why they were there, it turns out they were all waiting to be evacuated. Some have been staying here since yesterday. But the buses that arrived were not enough, and they were left to wait until the next day. People with children, dogs and things in early March, when it was still frosty at night, just spent the night on the street in order to get on the bus for evacuation. Evacuation buses were organized by volunteers, they contacted the military, found out exactly on that day where it was possible to drive and drove at their own peril and risk. A friend of mine went out with her mother with a child and she herself was pregnant. Only she and her child managed to get into the first minibus, and then they just sat on the floor in the truck and did not even know where they were going, because there were no windows in the car. There was no connection, it's good that they agreed with her mother to meet at the railway station in Kyiv in which case. And they really got to meet. It's hard to imagine even how they were driving, thank God everything is fine with her and the child.

When I was already driving up to the house, I met a woman with a dog whom I met in line in the first days of the war. She told me that they had no electricity and water for almost a week. And they go to take water just from our river, and the toilet was built on the street by the neighbors. I also thought, maybe I should tell her where we live so that she can come to get water, but I started thinking about how to explain to her and what to show, and in the end I didn't say anything. Now I reproach myself for this, but at that time I was really too confused, and did not know what to do. She also said that there has been no connection with her son, who serves in the army, for a long time and she had tears in her eyes, I did not even try to console her. How can you be comforted in a situation like that? We stood for another 10 minutes, discussing weekdays. She, too, wondered why our town wasn't on the news. After all, we are bombed every day, there are no more products in the stores, what's next? And there is not a word about Chernihiv in the news.

"Boom! Boom! Boom!" – somewhere not far away our artillery was working, so we need to go home, there will be an answer soon.

– God take care of you. – I said and rolled home.

We also heard the work of our artillery and also prepared for a response. We had already had dinner and quickly washed the dishes with either four hands. The dishes were now washed in two basins, in one with soapy water, in the other they were rinsed and then we poured the water into the yard. Yulia looked at her phone.

– They are announcing an air raid alert for the Chernihiv region, let's all quickly go to the basement, – she said and we went downstairs.

There was no electricity, the children were bored, not scared, only they didn't talk about it, only Nykon's eyes were running and when there was another explosion, they blinked heavily. Since my phone was still charged, I turned on the cartoon on my phone. And I myself began to communicate with Yulia and Yura. Yulia and Yura's parents lived in a remote area of the city, and since there was no connection for a long time, they did not know if everything was all right with them. After all, this is the outskirts of the city, the outskirts were bombed very heavily, Yura was worried:

– When they stop bombing, I'll go and visit my parents.

– By car?

– No, I want to have a full tank of gasoline left just in case, I may have to go somewhere. I'll take your bike, can I?

– You can, but it will be small for you. Vitya left his bike, better take it, it will be just the right size for you, only it will take an hour to go there.

– I'll try to be quick, but I need to go to see if everything is all right.

Only in the darkness did Nykon's voice sound:

– Mom, dad is calling.

I ran to the phone, it was very difficult to get a connection.

– Well, how are you? – Kostya immediately asked, probably it was not the first time that he tried to get through.

– They bomb around the clock, there is no electricity, the water is barely dripping, there is still food, but I don't know how long we will have enough. What should I do?

– We need to get out of the city. Leave everything, take the child and depart. Is there a possibility to leave?

– How? Our car is under repair. Maybe if one of my friends will go, but I don't know.

– I'll try to ask my friends, let's call each other later.

And he hung up.

When the bombing was stopped and it turned out that our house was intact again, Yura got on a bicycle and went to his parents. And I took the dogs and children and went to run to the river. But as soon as we reached the river, they started bombing again, it was very scary and we started back home with all our might. Without undressing we immediately hurried to the basement. Yulia was very worried, because Yura had gone to another area.

– Let's pray that everything will be fine, – I said and began to read the prayer. And then our mutual friend got through to me and offered to go to his country house near Kyiv, because it's calm there. But I refused, because I understood that it was calm today, but tomorrow the situation may change, I thanked him for caring, it's still nice that there are people who care about me and my children. Then, when we had already left, it was very hot near Kyiv, so it's good that I didn't agree.

And then other friends called, probably it was Kostya who tried to find a car for me. They left a few days before, went to Vinnitsa. Although they were not going to leave at all, when I called them before, they simply barricaded the windows with sandbags and sat in the apartment. But when the light and water went out, they nevertheless decided to leave, but they didn't invite me, because before that, when they called, I firmly said that I would not go anywhere. They said that if I went to Vinnitsa, they would take me away, at least for a while I would have somewhere to stay. When they arrived in Vinnitsa, the husband was immediately summoned to the draft board, but he is a priest. His wife was worried that he would be taken into the army, but I tried to reassure her that he was a priest and could not kill people, maybe they would take him as a military chaplain. Then I found out that he had come, but he was told that priests were not needed in the army, and he simply stayed there to live and serve in the local church.

Then Kostya phoned again and said that most of the friends he counted on had already left. But there still were several friends who had a car and he said that if they went, then they should pick me up, although everyone said that there was no green corridor and leaving now was more dangerous than staying in the city. Sobs were heard in the receiver, it was Tykhon who was crying next to him.

– Mommy, I'm very scared. I love you very much, I miss you, I want to see you. Please let daddy come to you.

– Son, dear, please stay there. We, most likely with Nykon, will try to come to you, but it is not yet known how.

This is where our conversation ended.

The bombardment ended, it began to get dark, but Yura was still not there. Yulia could not find a place for herself, she kept going from room to room, went several times to her house and began to prepare to put the children to bed. And then we heard the gate creak, we went out into the yard, it was Yura.

– Well, how was it? What was there? – Yulia almost screamed.

- They're in the basement. Both your parents and mine. I offered them to drive out in my car, so that dad could sit behind the wheel, put you all in and take you out, but they don't want to. They said that they would be in Chernihiv until the end, no matter what happened.

Yura put the bike in the shed and went into the house to eat. Yulia served him supper and sat next to him at the table under the flashlight to talk. I did not interfere with them, especially since it was already dark and it was possible to go to bed while it was quiet. I went down to the basement, checked how the children settled there, pulled a hat on Nykon, put on a winter jacket and boots, and also covered him with a blanket. In the basement it was already as cold as on the street, I did not dare to put the children in the house. They were bombing very hard now, and there was a possibility that at night they could get into our house, and it's one thing when you jump up and decide what to do yourself, and another thing when you jump up and don't know where to run with your child.

I once again gave the porridge to the dogs and cats, because Misha had already gone to bed, and went to his room. Passing by Nykon's room, I heard a baby crying outside the door. Masha and Yura decided to sleep upstairs, it was too dangerous for the baby to sleep in the cold basement. I went into the room and lay down under the covers, but before I had time to close my eyes, I heard blows on the battery. It was Yura again fiddling with the valve on the boiler. And it was like that every evening, but at least we had heating. A few minutes later the door to the room opened and Tom came in. Immediately, without asking, he jumped onto the bed and lay down on Kostya's side, I did not throw him off, he was probably also scared to stay on the floor under the window.

19. They came for us.

I opened my eyes at the sharp sound. Tom moved closer to me and hid his face between my neck and shoulder. Of course, I didn't scold him, but rather started scratching behind his ear, I was scared myself, but at least I understood what was happening. But the dog did not understand, he just heard sharp sounds and was afraid. The windows were trembling, they were bombing somewhere very close. I tried to close my eyes and put the headphones in my ears, but the explosions could be heard through the headphones too. I couldn't bring myself to close my eyes because it seemed to me that as soon as I closed them, the house would collapse. I got up and went to the kitchen to get some water. There, by a candle, mother sat:

– Can't sleep?

– Can't sleep.

– It's getting worse every day. You should try to take Nykon out of the city at least.

– Yes, I asked Kostya yesterday, but all our friends with cars had already left. Will you go if you have the opportunity?

– Not. I won't go. But Nykon needs to be taken away, it's not a thing for a child to sit in the basement for the third week, what will happen to his psyche then?

– How can I leave you? And the dog? What about the cat?

– Save the child. I will look after the house and the animals.

– What if something happens and I'm not around?

– What if something happens and you're upstairs? You will not be gone, and the children will become orphans. You will leave, we will have more food and there will be more space in the shelter.

– I will think. – I said, drank water with drops of Zelenin to calm the nervous system and went into the room. The bombing was over, but now the thoughts to go or not to go kept me awake. Deciding to go was very difficult. Yes, and how to go? Go stand in line for the evacuation to the first school? "I will think about it tomorrow". – I said to myself and fell asleep.

All this time I didn't dream. It felt like I was falling into darkness and emerging from there. Here and now, as if emerged from the darkness into the light. I got up mechanically, put on a sweater, put my phone in my pocket and went to the kitchen, and Tom ran after me. Fluffy stood up on her chair and arched her back. Everyone wanted to eat and go outside.

When everyone woke up and had breakfast, I called Nykon to walk the dogs. Dad went with Caesar, and Nykon and I went with Tom. It was a little cloudy, but it was still noticeable that spring was already coming. I started talking to Nykon about leaving the city. He didn't want to leave. But I told him that it's probably better, look, there's no electricity anymore and most likely there won't be, water is still dripping, but soon it won't be there either, if the gas pipe is damaged, then there will be no gas and then we will just stay in the stone, cold, dark bag.

– Where are we going? – Nykon then asked.

– I don't know, son. I just think it would be more correct to go immediately beyond the borders of Ukraine. It seems to me that on the territory of Ukraine we will not be able to be safe anywhere in the near future.

– And what about dad and Tykhon? – Nykon got excited.

– They can take care of themselves, don't worry, they're in a monastery. And as soon as the opportunity presents itself, they will immediately join us.

- Well, if you think it's better, let's go, and when?

– I don't know, let's pray that God will arrange it.

And we walked and prayed with Nykon that God would arrange our departure.

We returned home, and there was fuss, it turned out that Yura was again called to work. Yulia is in a panic again: they are bombing more and more, how will he work, and where will they hide in case of shelling? I immediately thought that there would be no one to bother with the heating boiler. I also thought that if the house suffered from shelling, then there would be no male power to dismantle these rubble. Only Yura was serious and collected, he was going to just go and do his job.

My dad and I decided to take the battery to their apartment for charging, and go shopping while it was quiet. While we were loading the battery, Tom kept walking around for us to take him with us. But it was impossible to take him with us, all the yards were strewn with broken glass and he could cut his paws. He was always so upset when we left, he had such a look, a human one.

The weather was wonderful, a real spring day. We put the battery on charge in the apartment, and went shopping and for a walk around the city. There were more people on the streets, everyone wanted to see spring.

Going out onto the main street, we met acquaintances – we hugged and almost cried. Alive! Do you understand? Alive! They lived far from the center and their shops were closed for a long time, and they decided to come to the center (about 1.5 hours to go) to get food. Since they were heavily shelled, they no longer had water, electricity or gas. They ate dry food, did not cook on a fire, went to the toilet outside. We decided to walk together along the central avenue. The snow had already melted, buds were swelling on the trees, flowers planted in autumn were visible in the flowerbeds. And everything seemed as always, until we reached the hotel "Ukraine". Friends became rooted to the spot and could not move for several seconds, only silently opened their mouths. Yes, the picture was really impressive. The hotel in the very center of Chernihiv was beautiful, but now there was no roof and middle part, only debris lay at the crossroads.

– Terrible. — They just uttered and we went on. When we got to the store, surprisingly, there was no queue, and the store was open. We went inside: there was twilight and people were sitting in this twilight and charging their phones. In those network adapters where refrigerators used to be plugged in, chargers with phones were now plugged in, people just sat on the shelves, on which there used to be potatoes and cereals. I will probably never forget this picture. It was eerie, as if the apocalypse had really come. We walked around the store, but there were absolutely no products, not even chips. Closer to the cash registers there were several shelves with shampoos, soap powder, but we did not need it, just like most people. Why buy shampoo and powder, if there is no water anyway?

Friends decided to go in the direction of another store, and my dad and I decided to go the other way, check my store and go to my old yard to call Shadow the cat. I still have photos from this walk, because it was surprisingly quiet and calm all that hour while we were walking. I traveled around the city almost every day, sometimes you need one thing or another, and I had already seen enough destruction, but for dad, of course, it was a shock. He kept sighing and swearing aloud, apparently he couldn't find the words. We walked past the pediatric dentistry, past the Shchers cinema, which no longer existed. Then, we went to another store, but the picture was the same as in the previous one. I would like to say thanks to the owner and director of the store, who opened it so that people could charge their phones. After all, they could just close the store, but they opened it and allowed people to use electricity without taking anything in return. Maybe they had some kind of backup line or generators, I don't know, but they had electricity.

We went further. When I went into the basement of the house where we used to live and called Shadow, he immediately ran out. I missed him so much, I was so worried that I pressed him to me, and he pressed against me and began to purr and rub his muzzle against my face. The girl Masha came out and cried, realizing that I was taking Shadow with me. And I stood in indecision, not knowing what to do. On the one hand, I missed him very much, and I also wanted to sleep next to him again, on the other hand, I felt sorry for the girl.

– Masha, don't worry, I'm not taking him away for good, he'll stay with me for a day and come running back to you.

– Well, take it now, don't torture the kid, she will calm down faster, – a man said unkindly.

I turned around and went away. Now I regret it, I should have left him, but I missed him very much. Shadow sat inside my shirt and murmured, he also missed me.

So we came home, me, dad and Shadow, we decided to go get the battery later. And when we were already approaching the house, I saw a neighbor who lives on the corner of the street, he knocked on the window.

– Hello. – I greeted him.

– Hi. We are leaving tomorrow at dawn, are you with us? – He immediately blurted out without further ado.

– Yes. – I answered without further ado. After all, Nykon and I made a decision in the morning and asked God for a blessing, and now He sends a person, so we need to go.

– Can you drive a car?

– Yes, a small one.

– Are you good at driving?

– I can drive around the city, but I don't often drive, usually my husband does the driving.

– It doesn't suit us. You will need to drive a big car and very fast, off-road, if you get confused, it may be trouble.

– If necessary, I can drive a big car.

– If I don't find anyone else, I'll take you. I'll come back tonight and tell you.

He turned around and walked towards his house. It was evidently nervous tension, he was very worried, but at the same time firmness and determination inspired confidence.

I went into the house and immediately told everyone:

– Nykon and I are leaving tomorrow. Who is with us? Decide now, and I'll go to get ready. – I said without any unnecessary delay and went to get a backpack. Shadow was forgotten, he was fed, of course, but there was no time for him, which is why I regret that I took him.

– How do you go? With whom? – Mom got excited.

– A neighbor round the corner. They drive several cars.

– Is there a green corridor?

– No. And there won't be any. You just need to trust God and go. Will you go? Maybe you'll change your mind?

– No. I decided to stay. Let's hope that the house survives and you will have somewhere to return. I'll bake pancakes for you in the morning. – Mom said and went to the kitchen. And I continued to get ready for the trip.

First of all, I put down a laptop – this is work and study and entertainment, if you need to be distracted. Charging for the phone and PowerBank. I took out the documents, there are a lot of them, but there is not enough space, and I just photographed what I might need on the road. I put the passports in the inner pocket of my jacket ... and once again said out loud: "I put the passports in the inner pocket of my jacket", in confusion you can put it somewhere and forget about it, it happened to me. The passports lay together: mine, Nykon's, Kostya's and Tykhon's. What to do? Can you take everything with you? Will you ever be able to get to them? And what if it doesn't work out, and they will need to go, but won't have passports? I decided to take only ours, mine and Nykon's. I showed my mother where the passports and money were if Kostya and Tykhon needed them. And added that if they needed money, they would take it without any questions.

Medicines. It was necessary to take something as a last resort, because this is a trip, it is not known what will be useful, and you can't take too much either. Knowing how other people left, I understood that we could stay somewhere in an open field, maybe at night, and it's still cold, but you can't take a lot, you need to be mobile, but you need to wear winter jackets so as not to freeze if something happens. I prepared clothes for myself and Nykon to put on in the morning and put spare pants and a T-shirt with me for myself and him. Well, in general, that was all, it was impossible to take more things, because it was necessary to take food and hot tea and coffee in thermoses. I was preparing for a situation where we would not be able to get out of Chernihiv region on the first day and would have to spend the night in a field in a car, or go on foot. And I also took a bandage and cotton wool, in case we get under fire and there are the wounded. I decided not to put the cord for charging the phone far away, if anything happens, I will use it as a tourniquet to stop bleeding.

I went into the kitchen, where Yulia was sitting holding her head:

– I don't know what to do, how can I go with two children? Anya will sit still, but Dima, he is two years old, he will not sit still.

– Well, I will help, you know that I will not leave you with two children.

– Yura also says we should go, but I will not dare anyway. He wanted my father to take us out in our car, but our car is low, it may not go along the fields, we will get stuck in the middle of the field.

Masha came out with a baby in her arms.

– Will you go?

– I'm not going by myself. May Yura go with us?

– Does Yura drive a car?

– No.

– I could ask, but most likely not. Men are allowed to leave the city only if they, as drivers, take their families out. Your baby is two weeks old, it's only getting worse. You have a few more hours to think. The neighbor will come before night, he will tell the details.

And I still had to decide about Misha so I called Anna.

– I'll be leaving. Should I leave Misha at home or take him with me? – and I told Anna how and with whom we will go. She still stayed near Kyiv.

– Leave him at your place. It will be better that way. Grandma will look after him. And I will look for an opportunity to come.

– All right if you say so. – I answered and went further to get ready, or rather to think to take some things or not to take.

Suddenly we got electricity. Electricians worked no matter what, honor and praise to them. Dad decided not to go for the battery, but leave it for the night to get fully charged.

The neighbor didn't come to us in the evening. Maybe it's all cancelled? To be honest, I didn't want to go anywhere. At home, everything is organized and everything is clear, but on the road there is only uncertainty. Maybe I should tell him I'm not going anywhere? What will he think of me? It makes no difference what he thinks, I've changed my mind and that's it. And if to act wisely, we need to go. It's hard and scary, but necessary.

I decided to put Nykon to sleep in my bed, so that in the morning I could immediately wake him up, and not go into the basement. But, as soon as he fell asleep, they started bombing, and I couldn't sleep, I kept thinking: should I take the child to the basement? It's good that we leave tomorrow. How long can you endure this horror? Hit or miss from day to day. This is not what the psyche can stand, so you can go crazy, you need to leave. We just need to survive a few days of the road, and we are safe – I firmly decided.

20. The road.

I woke up at 3 am. It was quiet, you could see the moon and stars through the window. "How nice!," – I thought. Where was I going to go? It is not known how it will end. The road is dangerous, there is no green corridor, both friends and foes are shooting, and in general a bunch of armed people is there, it is not known who you will run into. Nykon was snoring quietly next to me, and Tom was tossing and turning by the bed. I thought that even if a neighbor comes to us in the morning, I will say that I have changed my mind. Thank God, our house is well-built, the electricity is turned on, the river is nearby, if there are problems with water and food, we have stocked up, somehow we will survive. So I made a decision and fell asleep again.

"Boom! Boom!" – something howled again outside the window. I opened my eyes, Nykon sniffled, not reacting to anything. Boom, boom, boom – something exploded and collapsed. Nykon was lying closer to the window.

"Should I put him in my place?" – I thought. How scary! Not for myself, for the child. I tucked Nykon in. Every day the shelling was more and more frequent and closer to our house. What to do? I was confused again. I need to leave, I don't want to live like this! I put the headphones in my ears and fell asleep.

– Maria! Get up! It's already 6 o'clock, I've baked pancakes. – Mom looked into the room.

– I want to sleep!

– Get up. Now they will come for you, and you are sleeping.

– Maybe they won't. He didn't come in the evening. – I grumbled, but got up.

– Should it wake Nykon up?

– No. Maybe everything has been cancelled. Why worry the child?

I went to the kitchen, made myself some coffee and went to brush my teeth.

– They are knocking! Maria, there's a knock on the window! – mother Galya came running.

I spit out the paste into the wash basin.

– Lord have mercy, they came! – I wiped my mouth and ran to the window.

– We're leaving in ten minutes, – the neighbor said, turned around and left.

– We must go. – I told moms. - Mom Olya, dress Nykon. – I ordered, and she quickly began to pour coffee and tea into the thermoses.

I did not have time to change clothes, I went as I was, in trousers and a jacket, in which I had been sitting in the basement for a week. Later, when I washed and changed into clean clothes, I realized that my jacket, in which I was sitting in the basement, stinks. And so I went all the way, let people forgive such a neighborhood. I quickly packed pancakes, crackers, water and I turned around – Nikon is standing in a jacket, hat and sneakers, but with his eyes are closed - the child is sleeping. I also put on my shoes and dressed, prepared my backpacks and drank two sips of coffee, not more, it's not known when it will be possible to go to the toilet...

– Shall we sit down? – Mom said.

– Let's sit down. – I answered and we all sat down in the kitchen for a minute.

We have such a tradition to sit down for a minute before starting a trip, calm down, pray, and only then go. Tom came up and sat in front of me and began to look into my eyes so faithfully and devotedly, it seems to me that he understood everything, and kept waiting for the words "with me."

– I will definitely come back for you. – I told him, and I really believed in it, only he did not believe me.

We got up and went out into the yard, he ran alongside, and when we went out the gate, he kept trying to break through, but I closed him in the yard. Mom says that after our departure he lay down near the gate and did not want to eat or drink, he lay like that all day. The most devoted being in the world, I hope so much that we will meet again.

We came to the corner, the cars were already approaching there. Our convoy was of five cars, I was told to put things in one of them and stand aside for now until they decide who is driving and who is following whom. They decided not to take me as a driver, the neighbor put his wife behind the wheel, probably, he trusted her more. I asked my mother to write down the models and numbers of the cars, in case of emergency, and she did. I wonder how mom feels when she writes down the number of a car so she can identify it when it burns down. A few minutes later, a neighbor's voice sounded:

– Get in the cars!

We and our mothers hugged and I got into the car with Nykon. Almost immediately we set off, Nykon was still waving at the window to the grandmothers, and I silently began to read a prayer. Nykon was going through the city for the first time since the start of the war, and for him the checkpoints and destroyed houses were a new and interesting sight. He looked with admiration at the military with machine guns at checkpoints and with surprise at the destroyed apartments, then he also said that he would like to see a man with a machine gun again, I answered:

– Oh, son, it's better not to.

We quickly reached the outskirts of the city. On the outskirts of the city, near the broken car, there were people, and we picked them up, just there was a young guy who could drive well, and he got behind the wheel of our car. There were more cars at the exit and for some time we moved in one large column. We left the city, at first the path was along a regular road, until we crossed the automobile bridge over the Desna River. Here, most likely, there had already been battles, because we saw broken and burned tanks and armored personnel carriers. Almost immediately after the bridge the military showed us the way through the fields. The road was not paved, full of bumpy potholes, and at first our driver felt sorry for the suspension of the car and slowed down in some places, but the neighbor ran out of another car and shouted at him:

– Drive at top speed! You can drive here for an hour or two! You don't need to take care of the car, you need to take care of the lives of the people entrusted to you!

And he ran back to his car.

The driver shrugged his shoulders and stepped on the gas, and we rushed with the maximum possible speed along such a road. We were terribly shaking in the car, Nykon began to feel sick, I gave him a bag in case it got worse, and I continued to pray. And on the sides of this road there were abandoned cars with a low landing, like Yura's. No wonder he said that his car might not pass, indeed the road was difficult and those cars that could not pass were simply left on the side of the road. After some time, we again drove onto a normal road, but drove literally a kilometer along it and turned into the fields again, shaking began again, I asked Nykon to try to fall asleep, although how can you fall asleep here?

In the middle of the field we were stopped by the military:

– Where are you going? You can't come here anymore! Take to the left and try to pass there!

And the whole column moved to the left to try to pass further. Explosions were heard in the distance, it was very scary, I kept imagining tanks coming out from behind a hillock.

– Look at the plane! – the girl from the front seat pointed to the sky, and indeed there was a plane, I began to pray again, it was so scary that now it would turn around and start bombing us. But it apparently had more interesting targets. At the next checkpoint they turned us even more to the left, I sat and thought that at the next checkpoint we could be turned around at all, ordered to return to the city if there was an offensive. But after several hours of continuous shaking and nerves, we drove to the Kyiv highway. Only the Russian troops had been near Kyiv for a long time, and we probably drove along the highway no more than 5-10 kilometers, and again turned off the highway onto a country road. Somewhere between the villages our cars stopped:

– Go to the toilet, – sounded the voice of the neighbor.

I took Nykon's hand and was about to enter the forestation to hide behind a tree.

- Where are you going?! There are mines everywhere! Do it in front of the cars!

The neighbor was apparently very tense, he could not talk normally, he just yelled. It probably seemed obvious to him, but sitting in the basement I didn't know that everything around was mined. I sat right next to the car, and Nykon categorically refused to pee in front of everyone. I got angry, I wanted to yell at him too, but I began to persuade him:

– Look, adults are standing and doing it, no one is looking at anyone, and no one will look at you.

He still took two steps forward from the road, but he was stopped by the rumble of adults, because if he ran into a mine, then not only he would suffer, but the surrounding people too.

We got back into our cars and drove off. It was impossible to guess the names of some villages because the signs of settlements and bus stops were changed by the military in order to confuse Russian tankers. In one of the settlements we were turned around again and told to go through other villages, we returned about 3 km back and turned in the other direction, drove through another village. Shots and explosions were heard in the distance, but we continued to drive at the maximum possible speed.

When we drove past the fields, we saw signs "mines". How to sow grain in mined fields? This year there will definitely be a shortage of crops and high prices.

Finally, after about 5 hours of driving, we came to Kyiv. On the outskirts of the capital of Ukraine, there were few people and there were several destroyed houses, but when we drove closer to the center, I was very surprised. Cafes and shops were open, people were walking their dogs and drinking coffee. This picture really impressed me. After all, it seemed to me that the whole country was living in continuous tension, that they were bombing everywhere, that people were dying everywhere. Kyiv is a very big city, and while the outskirts were already bombed, people in the center could still continue to live a normal life.

We stopped at some gas station, everyone got out of the cars and started hugging. We made it, we got out!

There was coffee and some sweets with chocolates at the gas station, like a savage, I began to grab everything, then exhaled, put everything in its place, took coffee and some kind of cookie to Nykon, but it was like in a fairy tale.

– Do you have money? Can you fill up the car? – the neighbor came up to me.

– Yes, I do. Of course I will.

And I went to the checkout.

I know that if I hadn't had money, they would have taken me anyway. But, I had money, and it's even good that he offered me to fill up the car, so I could feel that I was participating in a common cause, and not just sitting. There was gas at the gas stations here, and there was not even a long queue, which was also amazing. We drank coffee, chatted and got back into our cars. Now we have to leave Kyiv. Only one road was accessible to the south from Kyiv, and it was shot through from both sides. But then everything was quiet. We drove mostly along paved roads and often along highways, only checkpoints between cities reminded us of the war.

We drove through Bila Tserkva, this city had not yet been bombed. People lived their normal lives as if nothing was happening in the rest of the country. I remembered how we lived eight years ago, when the war began in the east. Yes, we took my mother away, we were worried, we watched the news, "what if it comes to us." But in general, we continued to live our normal lives, walking, drinking coffee, working, making plans. There is a war in the country, but until the bombs fall on your head, it seems that this does not concern you. I think the whole world is now living the same way, somewhere in distant Ukraine there is a war going on, what a pity that people are dying, but this does not concern us.

During one of the stops, the neighbor's wife handed out sandwiches to everyone. She made them for everyone, you know, for all five cars. What good fellows they are! They gathered, organized people, found gasoline, prepared sandwiches! Not everyone can do that. They began to discuss a hotel in Vinnitsa, I said that, generally, I don't care, I'll go where everybody goes, and if you book rooms, then count Nykon and me, one bed is enough for us if there are not enough places.

We again got into the cars and an hour and a half later we were already in Vinnitsa. Here life went on as usual. No blackout, no curfew, life went on. We arrived at the hotel and rented rooms. Nykon and I settled with another woman in a double room, we really got one bed, but this is not a problem, we will sleep safely.

But suddenly, an air raid alarm howled, we all shuddered, began to look at each other. The women came up to the reception and asked:

– Where is the bomb shelter?

– We have a basement, we brought some chairs there. You can go down there if you like.

–What do you mean saying "if you like"? – We didn't understand. And then we understood. They haven't been bombed yet. They don't know what it is. They haven't been in basements yet. They were said to equip the shelter, they equipped it – they brought chairs to the basement.

We went up to the room, had a snack, and went to bed almost immediately. I thought that I would finally sleep peacefully all night and get enough sleep, and I would not get up in the morning until nine. But at 6 in the morning I opened my eyes out of habit, the spring sun looked in the window, and the birds chirped. I got up and went downstairs to look for coffee. It turned out that there were bowls with cookies and sweets at the entrance, there was a kettle, water and free tea and coffee. Many people left the hot territories through Vinnitsa, and this is how they expressed their support.

A friend called me:

– Maria, we left yesterday. How are you?

– We also left. Where are you?

– We are in Vinnitsa. Imagine, here on the ground floor they prepared cookies and tea for us, they feel sorry for us.

– What hotel are you in? – I looked at the tea and cookies. – Come on, get downstairs.

It's amazing, but my friends who were going to go to my shelter saw a convoy of cars and decided to try to get out of the city, and they succeeded just like us. Most likely, we even rode in one large column. He came down, we hugged and almost burst into tears. I think Kostya asked him to take us out if they were leaving, but he saw the convoy and left himself, probably it bothered him. But over all of us there is God and He corrected everything in the way that is best for everyone.

– How about your wife? Will she come downstairs?

– She is washing now, maybe later. Can you imagine it: we'll have a baby! We've been waiting for this for so long! Imagine, on February, 28, my wife brings me a pregnancy test with two strips, and we are already sitting in the basement, and being bombed every day. I went out into the street, I walk around the city and cry and I don't know whether to rejoice or grieve.

– Rejoice, of course! Now everything will be fine! The Lord will not leave you! Take care of your wife! I'm so happy for you! – I hugged him again, it was so touching. Thank God that they decided to leave when they saw the convoy.

The neighbor came down and I went to ask what their plans were. They were going to go to the western part of Ukraine, and they had an agreement about an apartment, but the owners of the apartment stopped responding. Then it was very difficult with apartments in western Ukraine, but they agreed for a normal price, perhaps the owners decided that it was too cheap. I, God forgive me, condemn these homeowners. Answer the phone, say that you won't rent out or say that you will do it, but it's more expensive, let people decide for themselves. And the neighbors decided to stay in Vinnitsa for one or two more days. I had nothing to do in Vinnitsa, I immediately decided that I would leave the country, and so I went to the railway station to wait for the train to the west.

21. After.

There were no trains at all. We stood on the platform and did not know what to do next. And then we met a woman with a child, she was going to the Czech Republic, and she suggested taking a bus to Warsaw, but for money. The same buses that the workers used continued to run on schedule. We arrived at the bus station, and it turned out that there were just 4 seats on the next bus, of course we bought them.

When we were driving to Warsaw at night, I couldn't sleep. And I visited websites where people who could accept Ukrainian refugees published offers. I studied English at school, although I didn't remember anything, but that's why I poked into England. I looked at the offers and put the phone in my pocket, not daring to do anything. And then I decided: I'll just write, I'll try, and see if it works out or not. I answered the ad that somehow attracted me, added a link to Facebook so that people knew who was writing to them, and again tried to sleep.

I couldn't sleep. I myself with a child at six in the morning will find myself in a foreign country, what should I do next? I reached for the phone again and saw that they answered me from Britain that they were waiting for us. It was so unexpected and scary. Some man from Britain is ready to accept a woman with a child – suspicious. But then he said that he also had two sons and he would pass on my contact to his wife, and she would do the paperwork, and I calmed down a bit. When we arrived in Warsaw, I already knew that I would go to Britain.

All this time, a friend from Lviv contacted me, she helped other people to leave and called to tell me that we could spend the night at hers if necessary. It turned out differently, but she advised me to go to a camp for migrants near Warsaw and rest there for a couple of days and recover, and I did just that. The Poles, of course, surprised us with their attention and hospitality, care for the little things, we were literally carried in their arms to eat, to the toilet and onto the bus.

We arrived at the refugee camp, it was a huge hangar with a bunch of folding beds, everyone was given a blanket, a pillow, and shampoo and toothpaste if needed. Nykon and I washed and changed into clean clothes. After that we went to a makeshift kitchen, drank coffee and cocoa. But only I was somehow not myself, I did not like this place. By 10 o'clock a queue began to form near the kitchen, I asked:

– Is there not enough food?

– Enough. There are even leftovers.

I did not understand. Nykon and I went to look around, and it turned out that buses to different European countries leave from another hangar. The nearest bus departed for the Netherlands and I decided to go right away, still closer to England if everything works out. So we went to the Netherlands at night and we were assigned to different people, they put us in cars and took us somewhere at night. There were so many fears, because we are powerless creatures in a foreign country, without even knowing the language. I was afraid that they would take me to some village and force me to work and be raped and abused. But we ended up with wonderful people Maria and Bert. They gave Ukrainian refugees the whole house where her parents once lived. I have no words to describe what wonderful, kind and caring people they were to treat us like close relatives. We stayed with them for a month while waiting for a visa to England.

It was necessary to pick up the rest of the family, and I began to persuade the grandmothers to leave. It is very difficult to run the process from abroad, but we succeeded.

Mom Galya went with Misha to the monastery to Kostya, and then from there, together with Tykhon, to Kyiv. They took Anna away and came to me in the Netherlands. Their journey lasted about five days, and it was very difficult, but I will not discribe it here. I was so nervous that I thought I would not survive those days. It's one thing when you're around and quite another when you can't do anything and can't help.

A few days after I left, they blew up the bridge across the Desna River, cutting off the path to the south. People continued to get out of the city, but it was already much more difficult.

When the troops left Chernihiv, my husband Kostya returned to the city, and since he was a doctor by profession, he went to serve in order to help people.

When there was a danger that the Russian troops would return, we decided that my mother would go to her sister in Moldova and take Tom the dog there, because Kostya served and it would be difficult for him to take care of him. But Tom became very ill two days before the departure, I constantly called the veterinarian from the Netherlands, my mother went by taxi to the veterinarian almost every day to save the dog. On the day of departure, Kostya persuaded me not to take Tom away, because he was still weak, but to leave him with him. In fact, it was the right decision, because now they serve together, and Kostya has a loving creature to cheer him up. Tom doesn't leave Kostya for a single moment. God take care of them.

Yura took Shadow the cat back to the bomb shelter the day after my departure. When the occupation ended, he stayed to live in my old yard, I contact the people living there by phone, they say that he eats well, everyone loves him.

And Fluffy the cat became a mother, because there was no one to have her sterilized under those conditions. And now she has two kittens.

Lena with her husband and children are now in Belgium, they are doing well. Both found work, the children go to school. I really want to visit them, but there is no way.

Kostya allowed volunteers to live in both apartments of his parents, and a family who had no housing also came to our house.

My Mom's cat Dymka and Aunt Tanya's cat Milka died after my departure. Nobody knows what happened to them. They died very quickly, in just two days, first one, then the other.

Hamster Shlepa died, although he was fed, but one day it turned out that he had died. Probably without children's attention and affection they do not live.

Aunt Tanya never went to her son and is still in Chernihiv, my mother became very good friends with her during the occupation and they now keep in touch via the Internet.

Both Yuras took their families with children out of Chernihiv a few days after I left, but now they have already returned to Chernihiv. Their wives don't want to go abroad without their husbands, and it's expensive to live in another city in Ukraine. So they live with constant sirens and the expectation that everything will start from the beginning. I warned that if the Russian troops start the offensive again, then my basement is open.

I persuaded my father to go to the Netherlands to live with his wife, and now they, along with Anna and Misha, live in a house provided by Maria and Bert.

As for dad's dog, Caesar, he is watched by a guy who lives in their apartment.

And I am with my two sons Tykhon and Nykon in the UK. We live with wonderful people, Kavita and Sunil. They not only let us into their home, they let us into their lives. It was unexpected for me that someone cares and helps me, because I'm used to doing everything myself, people usually turned to me for help. And now I am learning to ask for help if I need something and to accept help with gratitude. Our sponsors fiddled with us so much, they helped so much, Kavita even went to find me a job! And it was her idea to write a book when she realized that I was still in the basement in my head. I feel huge gratitude to these people, but because of the poor English, there are not enough words to express it to them, I only say: Thank you!

I work in a sports store, it's natural, it's easier without knowing the language as I already know what to do. The kids go to school and play football, they just miss their friends.

And everything seems normal from the outside, but nothing is normal. My feelings are frozen, I do not realize half of what is happening to me. When I wake up in the middle of the night, I can't figure out where I am. I live someone else's life, and mine stayed in my house with my husband and dog...

This could not be imagined. Ukraine.

Content.

1. The day before.

We just lived our lives... We went to work and the kids went to school. Tykhon and Kostya went to the monastery. Nykon and I went to a friend's birthday party. We were warned that within 48 hours there would be a full-scale Russian invasion, but we did not believe it.

2. Start.

Morning missile strikes. I don't believe it. Lena and neighbors come to me. The first bombings in the basement. Very cold.

3. Day two.

Children are walking in the courtyard of the house. Vitya has arrived. I was looking for open stores. Olya's mother came. Kostya called, asked to read the 90th psalm. Neighbors collect bottles for Molotov cocktails. Yulia's dad came in, he was at the recruiting station. Blackout.

4. Trip around the city.

Children build defenses in the yard. The first time I stood in line at the store in the morning. Went to another area of the city for the key. They blew up the building of the SBU. Mom Galya and aunt Tanya came. Lena's promise to wash me before burial. People order shoes online.

5. Bomb the city.

Another line to the store. A bag of sugar broke. At night, a rocket hit the parents' house. Lena's mother called and said that tanks were moving through the city. Dad came. Yura and Vitya are preparing axes. They took water.

6. The city is surrounded.

The children got sick. Yura wired the Internet to the basement. Collected winter shoes for the military. The Epicenter supermarket was blown up. She cooked liver for the dogs, and Galya's mother said to feed the children. Yura went to work, I told him to come back alive. They bombed all night. The children slept upstairs. Meeting with a friend Zhenya, as he got out of the city.

7. We clog windows.

We went to block the windows, we didn't pass the first time, we stopped at a checkpoint. The children slept upstairs. I saw a friend with a gun. It's a shame that street signs are being torn down. The news came about the dead in friends. Oksana and Kostya feed the elderly. Vitya and tobacco. Found spoiled food.

8. Rusks.

My mother and I went to the queue at the general store and got bread. Grandmothers Galya and Tanya went to Aunt Tanya's house. We walked the dogs with Lena. She persuaded me to go to the store - they started shooting. They cut Nykon's hair and the rest of the men. Very poor connection. We use the Internet in the basement. Bicycle legs buzz.

9. Grandmothers get sick.

When they bombed, I did not want to go down, Tom covered me with him. Went to the field for a walk with the dogs. Grandmothers got sick. I called to find out if Nykona was ready for a birthday present, no answer. Found flour. Turned off the light.

10. The cat ran away.

A friend said they blew up my store. Grandmothers continue to get sick. There are few medicines. Shadow ran away. Volunteers came, brought toys, I hid them for Nykon. Dad made crackers. I saw a line for cigarettes.

11. Changed shoes for medicines.

Garbage sweepers drive around the city. I traveled around the city looking for medicines, I did not find it. I changed shoes for medicines. While driving, someone did not check the barrel in the toilet, the pit overflowed. Vitya scoops up the hole with buckets. Julia saw how the plane was shot down. Nastya called and said that she got buckwheat.

12. Our area is being bombed.

Nykon learned a new song on the guitar. School 19 was bombed in the evening. I haven't changed my clothes for a long time - I went to wash. I persuaded grandmothers to wash, gave out clothes to everyone. Arranged a disco with the children during the day. Fluffy got sick. Lena's brother came with a machine gun, didn't let the house in. My sister called from Russia.

13. Nykon's birthday.

Wrote an application for a new mail about the transfer of money. Went to my mom to clean up. Found a working ATM. Nykon has a birthday. Kostya and Oksana arrived and brought a cake. Fluff continues to hurt. I saw people evacuating at the first school. Lena went home to spend the night.

14. Lena gets out of the city.

International Women's Day. The boys drew pictures and congratulated us. Wrote a post about the fact that the cat Shadow ran away. Fluff is recovering. When they were walking with Tom, the shelling began, he was very scared. Withdrawn money from an ATM for grandmothers, they wanted to share with me.

15. There is no more electricity.

Yura brought the battery, but he sat down until the evening. With difficulty they started the boiler for the night. We heard the tanks moving in the next street. She asked to work in a hospital. Tom is coming with me, he was afraid of gunshots when they were walking. Sold sneakers to a passerby. People cook food outside and build toilets.

16. People collect water in the river.

Communication almost does not work. We went to charge the battery. Yura and Masha called with a request to come to us. Zhenya told how he went to the dentist, he was caught put a bag on his head. I learned that Shadow was in a bomb shelter, they asked him to leave. Went to visit Ira. Think of animals as food.

17. New settlers.

Yura and Masha came. They smashed the Gagarin stadium. We walked by the river Yura and Dima walked too. Neighbor Yura went to his parents because there is no connection. There is no electricity. The water barely flows. Volunteers came to fetch water. We went to charge the battery - accidentally bought eggs. Caesar brought chicken. Kostya told me that Tykhon was going to visit me from the monastery. Lena told how they settled in Poland.

18. Bombed Ukraine.

I went home to charge my phone, the guard did not let me through the library. I met a friend in turn with a dog. Why is our city silent in the news. People are building toilets on the street. Gave shoes to volunteers. Misha called and offered to go to his dacha near Kyiv because it's calm there. Sophia called, they left, Artyom was summoned to the military registration and enlistment office. There are even more people near the first school, they spend the night there.

19. They came for us.

In the morning, walking with Nykon and with the dogs, they prayed that if we need to leave, let the Lord arrange everything. My dad and I went for a walk around the city, looking for shops that have groceries. Stores only charge phones. Met friends. Products not found. Found a cat Tenya. In the evening, a neighbor came by. Julia and Masha at the crossroads do not know whether to go or not. The documents. Anya called, what to do with Misha.

20. Road.

At night there were thoughts to leave or not to leave. Pancakes and coffee in the morning. Didn't have time to change. The road through the fields at speed. Kyiv that lives. Vinnytsia, which has not yet been bombed. Tom was refusing to eat when he realized that we had left.

21. After.

We left Vinnitsa by bus. I couldn't sleep on the bus, she wrote to Sunil. Warsaw, center for migrants. Bus to the Netherlands. Just great people. The cats are dead.